ISBN: 9781290518260

Published by:
HardPress Publishing
8345 NW 66TH ST #2561
MIAMI FL 33166-2626

Email: info@hardpress.net
Web: http://www.hardpress.net

MEMOIRS

OF

A REVOLUTIONIS[T]

BY

P. KROPOTKIN

WITH A PREFACE BY GEORGE BRANDES

IN TWO VOLUMES—VOL. I.

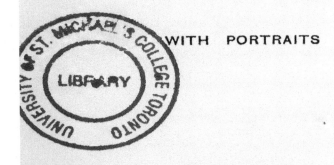

WITH PORTRAITS

LONDON

SMITH, ELDER, & CO., 15 WATERLOO PLACE

1899

PREFACE

THE Autobiographies which we owe to great minds
have in former times generally been of one of three
types : ' So far I went astray, thus I found the true
path ' (St. Augustine) ; or, ' So bad was I, but who
dares to consider himself better ! ' (Rousseau) ; or,
' This is the way a genius has slowly been evolved
from within and by favourable surroundings ' (Goethe).
In these forms of self-representation the author is thus
mainly pre-occupied with himself.

In the nineteenth century the autobiographies of
men of mark are more often shaped on lines such as
these : ' So full of talent and attractive was I ; such
appreciation and admiration I won ! ' (Johanne Louise
Heiberg, ' A Life lived once more in Reminiscence ') ;
or, ' I was full of talent and worthy of being loved,
but yet I was unappreciated, and these were the hard
struggles I went through before I won the crown of
fame ' (Hans Christian Andersen, ' The Tale of a
Life '). The main pre-occupation of the writer, in
these two classes of life-records, is consequently with

what his fellow-men have thought of him and said about him.

The author of the autobiography before us is not pre-occupied with his own capacities, and consequently describes no struggle to gain recognition. Still less does he care for the opinions of his fellow-men about himself ; what others have thought of him, he dismisses with a single word.

There is in this work no gazing upon one's own image. The author is not one of those who willingly speak of themselves ; when he does so, it is reluctantly and with a certain shyness. There is here no confession that divulges the inner self, no sentimentality, and no cynicism. The author speaks neither of his sins nor of his virtues ; he enters into no vulgar intimacy with his reader. He does not say when he fell in love, and he touches so little upon his relations with the other sex, that he even omits to mention his marriage, and it is only incidentally we learn that he is married at all. That he is a father, and a very loving one, he finds time to mention just once in the rapid review of the last sixteen years of his life.

He is more anxious to give the psychology of his contemporaries than of himself; and one finds in his book the psychology of Russia : the official Russia and the masses underneath—Russia struggling forward and Russia stagnant. He strives to tell the story of his contemporaries rather than his own ; and consequently, the record of his life contains the history of Russia during his lifetime, as well as that of the labour move-

ment in Europe during the last half-century. When
he plunges into his own inner world, we see the outer
world reflected in it.

There is, nevertheless, in this book an effect such
as Goethe aimed at in ' Dichtung und Wahrheit,' the
representation of how a remarkable mind has been
shaped ; and in analogy with the ' Confessions ' of St.
Augustine, we have the story of an inner crisis which
corresponds with what in olden times was called ' con-
version.'   In fact, this inner crisis is the turning point
and the core of the book.

There are at this moment only two great Russians
who think for the Russian people, and whose thoughts
belong to mankind, Leo Tolstoy and Peter Kropotkin.
Tolstoy has often told us, in poetical shape, parts of his
life.   Kropotkin gives us here, for the first time, without any poetical recasting, a rapid survey of his whole
career.

However radically different these two men are,
there is one parallel which can be drawn between
the lives and the views on life of both.   Tolstoy is
an artist, Kropotkin is a man of science ; but there
came a period in the career of each of them, when
neither could find peace in continuing the work
to which he had brought great inborn capacities.
Religious considerations led Tolstoy, social considerations led Kropotkin, to abandon the paths they had
first taken.

Both are filled with love for mankind ; and they
are at one in the severe condemnation of the indif-

ference, the thoughtlessness, the crudeness and brutality
of the upper classes, as well as in the attraction they
both feel towards the life of the downtrodden and ill-
used man of the people.   Both see more cowardice than
stupidity in the world.   Both are idealists and both
have the reformer's temperament.   Both are peace-
loving natures, and Kropotkin is the more peaceful of
the two—although Tolstoy always preaches peace and
condemns those who take right into their own hands
and resort to force, while Kropotkin justifies such
action, and was on friendly terms with the Terrorists.
The point upon which they differ most is in their
attitudes towards the intelligent educated man and
towards science altogether ; Tolstoy, in his religious
passion, disdains and disparages the man equally with
the thing, while Kropotkin holds both in high esteem,
although at the same time he condemns men of science
for forgetting the people and the misery of the masses.

Many a man and many a woman have accomplished
a great life-work without having led a great life.
Many people are interesting, although their lives may
have been quite insignificant and commonplace.   Kropotkin's life is both great and interesting.

In these volumes will be found a combination of
all the elements out of which an intensely eventful life
is composed—idyll and tragedy, drama and romance.

The childhood in Moscow and in the country, the
portraits of his mother, sisters, and teachers, of the old
and trusty servants, together with the many pictures of
patriarchal life, are done in such a masterly way that

every heart will be touched by them. The landscapes,
the story of the unusually intense love between the
two brothers—all this is pure idyll.

Side by side there is, unhappily, plenty of sorrow
and suffering: the harshness in the family life, the
cruel treatment of the serfs, and the narrow-minded-
ness and heartlessness which are the ruling stars of
men's destinies.

There is variety and there are dramatic cata-
strophes : life at Court and life in prison ; life in the
highest Russian society, by the side of emperors and
grand dukes, and life in poverty, with the working
proletariat, in London and in Switzerland. There
are changes of costume as in a drama ; the chief actor
having to appear during the day in fine dress in the
Winter Palace, and in the evening in peasant's clothes
in the suburbs, as a preacher of revolution. And
there is, too, the sensational element that belongs to
the novel. Although nobody could be simpler in tone
and style than Kropotkin, nevertheless parts of his
narrative, from the very nature of the events he has to
tell, are more intensely exciting than anything in those
novels which aim only at being sensational. One
reads with breathless interest the preparations for the
escape from the hospital of the fortress of St. Paul
and St. Peter, and the bold execution of the plan.

Few men have moved, as Kropotkin did, in all
layers of society ; few know all these layers as he does.
What a picture ! Kropotkin as a little boy with curled
hair, in a fancy-dress costume, standing by the Emperor

Nicholas, or running after the Emperor Alexander as his page, with the idea of protecting him. And then again—Kropotkin in a terrible prison, sending away the Grand Duke Nicholas, or listening to the growing insanity of a peasant who is confined in a cell under his very feet.

He has lived the life of the aristocrat and of the worker; he has been one of the Emperor's pages and a poverty-stricken writer; · he has lived the life of the student, the officer, the man of science, the explorer of unknown lands, the administrator, and the hunted revolutionist. In exile he has had at times to live upon bread and tea as a Russian peasant; and he has been exposed to espionage and assassination plots like a Russian emperor.

Few men have had an equally wide field of experience. Just as Kropotkin is able, as a geologist, to survey prehistoric evolution for hundreds of thousands of years past, so too he has assimilated the whole historical evolution of his own times. To the literary and scientific education which is won in the study and in the university (such as the knowledge of languages, belles-lettres, philosophy, and higher mathematics), he added at an early stage of his life that education which is gained in the workshop, in the laboratory, and in the open field—natural science, military science, fortification, knowledge of mechanical and industrial processes. His intellectual equipment is universal.

What must this active mind have suffered when he was reduced to the inactivity of prison life! What a test of endurance and what an exercise in stoicism ! Kropotkin says somewhere that a morally developed personality must be at the foundation of every organization. That applies to him. Life has made of him one of the corner-stones for the building of the future.

The crisis in Kropotkin's life has two turning-points which must be mentioned.

He approaches his thirtieth year—the decisive year in a man's life. With heart and soul he is a man of science ; he has made a valuable scientific discovery. He has found out that the maps of Northern Asia are incorrect ; that not only the old conceptions of the geography of Asia are wrong, but that the theories of Humboldt are also in contradiction with the facts. For more than two years he has plunged into laborious research. Then, suddenly, on a certain day, the true relations of the facts flash upon him ; he understands that the main lines of structure in Asia are not from north to south or from west to east, but from the south-west to the north-east. He submits his discovery to test, he applies it to numerous separated facts, and—it holds its ground. Thus he knew the joy of scientific revelation in its highest and purest form, he has felt how elevating is its action on the mind.

Then comes the crisis. The thought that these joys are the lot of so few, fills him now with sorrow. He asks himself whether he has the right to enjoy this knowledge alone—for himself. He feels that there is a higher duty before him—to do his part in bringing to the mass of the people the information already gained, rather than to work at making new discoveries.

For my part I do not think that he was right. With such conceptions Pasteur would not have been the benefactor of mankind that he has been. After all, everything, in the long run, is to the benefit of the mass of the people. I think that a man does the utmost for the well-being of all when he has given to the world the most intense production of which he is capable. But this fundamental notion is characteristic of Kropotkin; it contains his very essence.

And this attitude of mind carries him farther. In Finland, where he is going to make a new scientific discovery, as he comes to the idea—which was heresy at that time—that in prehistoric ages all Northern Europe was buried under ice, he is so much impressed with compassion for the poor, the suffering, who often know hunger in their struggle for bread, that he considers it his highest, absolute duty to become a teacher and helper of the great working and destitute masses.

Soon after that a new world opens before him— the life of the working classes—and he *learns* from those whom he intends to *teach*.

Five or six years later this crisis appears in its second phase. It happens in Switzerland. Already during his first stay there Kropotkin had abandoned the group of state-socialists, from fear of an economical despotism, from hatred of centralization, from love for the freedom of the individual and the commune: Now, however, after his long imprisonment in Russia, during his second stay amidst the intelligent workers of West Switzerland, the conception which floated before his eyes of a new structure of society, more distinctly dawns upon him in the shape of a society of federated associations, co-operating in the same way as the railway companies, or the postal departments of separate countries co-operate. He knows that he cannot dictate to the future the lines which it will have to follow ; he is convinced that all must grow out of the constructive activity of the masses, but he compares, for the sake of illustration, the coming structure with the guilds and the mutual relations which existed in mediæval times, and were worked out from below. He does not believe in the distinction between leaders and led ; but I must confess that I am old-fashioned enough to feel pleased when Kropotkin, by a slight inconsistency, says once in praise of a friend that he was ' a born leader of men.'

The author describes himself as a Revolutionist, and he is surely quite right in so doing. But seldom have there been revolutionists so humane and mild. One feels astounded when, in alluding on one occasion to the possibility of an armed conflict with the Swiss police, there appears in his character the fighting instinct which exists in all of us. He cannot say precisely in this passage whether he and his friends felt a relief at being spared a fight, or a regret that the fight did not take place. This expression of feeling stands alone. He has never been an avenger, but always a martyr.

He does not impose sacrifices upon others ; he makes them himself. All his life he has done it, but in such a way that the sacrifice seems to have cost him nothing. So little does he make of it. And with all his energy he is so far from being vindictive, that of a disgusting prison doctor he only remarks : ‘ The less said of him the better.’

He is a revolutionist without emphasis and without emblem. He laughs at the oaths and ceremonies with which conspirators bind themselves in dramas and operas. This man is simplicity personified. In character he will bear comparison with any of the fighters for freedom in all lands. None have been more disinterested than he, none have loved mankind more than he does.

But he would not permit me to say in the forefront of his book all the good that I think of him, and should I say it, my words would outrun the limits of, a reasonable Preface.

GEORGE BRANDES.

CONTENTS

OF

THE FIRST VOLUME

THIS book would not probably have been written for some time to come, were it not for the kind invitation and the most friendly encouragement of the editor and the publisher of the 'Atlantic Monthly' to write it for serial publication in their Review. I feel it a pleasant duty to acknowledge here my very best thanks both for the hospitality that was offered to me, and for the friendly pressure that was exercised in order to induce me to undertake this work. It was published in the 'Atlantic Monthly' (September 1898 to September 1899) under the title of 'Autobiography of a Revolutionist.' Preparing it now for publication in book form, I have considerably added to the original text in the portions relating to my youth and my stay in Siberia, and especially in the Sixth Part, in which I have narrated my life in Western Europe.

P. K.

October 1899.

PART FIRST

CHILDHOOD

I

Moscow is a city of slow historical growth, and down to the present time its different parts have wonderfully well retained the features which have been stamped upon them in the slow course of history. The Trans-Moskva River district, with its broad, sleepy streets and its monotonous gray painted, low-roofed houses, of which the entrance-gates remain securely bolted day and night, has always been the secluded abode of the merchant class, and the stronghold of the outwardly austere, formalistic, and despotic Nonconformists of the 'Old Faith.' The citadel, or Kreml is still the stronghold of Church and State; and the immense space in front of it, covered with thousands of shops and warehouses, has been for centuries a crowded beehive of commerce, and still remains the heart of a great internal trade which spreads over the whole surface of the vast empire. The Tverskáya and the Smiths' Bridge have been for hundreds of years the chief centres for the fashionable shops; while the artisans' quarters, the Pluschíkha and the Dorogomílovka, retain the very same features which characterized their uproarious populations in the times of the Moscow Tsars. Each quarter is a little world in itself; each has its own physiognomy, and lives its own separate life. Even the railways, when they made an irruption into the old capital, grouped apart in special centres on the outskirts of the old town their stores and machine-works and their heavily loaded carts and engines.

However, of all parts of Moscow, none, perhaps, is more typical than that labyrinth of clean, quiet, winding streets and lanes which lies at the back of the Kreml, between two great radial streets, the Arbát and the Prechístenka, and is still called the Old Equerries' Quarter —the Stáraya Konyúshennaya.

Some fifty years ago, there lived in this quarter, and slowly died out, the old Moscow nobility, whose names were so frequently mentioned in the pages of Russian history before the time of Peter I., but who subsequently disappeared to make room for the new-comers, 'the men of all ranks'—called into service by the founder of the Russian state. Feeling themselves supplanted at the St. Petersburg court, these nobles of the old stock retired either to the Old Equerries' Quarter in Moscow, or to their picturesque estates in the country round about the capital, and they looked with a sort of contempt and secret jealousy upon the motley crowd of families which came 'from no one knew where' to take possession of the highest functions of the government, in the new capital on the banks of the Nevá.

In their younger days most of them had tried their fortunes in the service of the state, chiefly in the army; but for one reason or another they had soon abandoned it, without having risen to high rank. The more successful ones obtained some quiet, almost honorary position in their mother city—my father was one of these—while most of the others simply

retired from active service. But wheresoever they
might have been shifted, in the course of their careers,
over the wide surface of Russia, they always somehow
managed to spend their old age in a house of their
own in the Old Equerries' Quarter, under the shadow
of the church where they had been baptized, and
where the last prayers had been pronounced at the
burial of their parents.

New branches budded from the old stocks. Some
of them achieved more or less distinction in different
parts of Russia; some owned more luxurious houses in
the new style in other quarters of Moscow or at St.
Petersburg; but the branch which continued to reside
in the Old Equerries' Quarter, somewhere near to the
green, the yellow, the pink, or the brown church
which was endeared through family associations, was
considered as the true representative of the family, irrespective of the position it occupied in the family tree.
Its old-fashioned head was treated with great respect,
not devoid, I must say, of a slight tinge of irony, even
by those younger representatives of the same stock who
had left their mother city for a more brilliant career in
the St. Petersburg Guards or in the court circles. He
personified, for them, the antiquity of the family and
its traditions.

In these quiet streets, far away from the noise and
bustle of the commercial Moscow, all the houses had
much the same appearance. They were mostly built
of wood, with bright green sheet-iron roofs, the
exteriors stuccoed and decorated with columns and
porticoes; all were painted in gay colours. Nearly
every house had but one story, with seven or nine big,

gay-looking windows facing the street. A second story was admitted only in the back part of the house, which looked upon a spacious yard, surrounded by numbers of small buildings, used as kitchens, stables, cellars, coach-houses, and as dwellings for the retainers and servants. A wide gate opened upon this yard, and a brass plate on it usually bore the inscription, 'House of So-and-So, Lieutenant or Colonel, and Commander' —very seldom 'Major-General' or any similarly elevated civil rank. But if a more luxurious house, embellished by a gilded iron railing and an iron gate, stood in one of those streets, the brass plate on the gate was sure to bear the name of 'Commerce Counsel' or 'Honourable Citizen' So-and-So. These were the intruders, those who came unasked to settle in this quarter, and were therefore ignored by their neighbours.

No shops were allowed in these select streets, except that in some small wooden house, belonging to the parish church, a tiny grocer's or greengrocer's shop might have been found; but then, the policeman's lodge stood on the opposite corner, and in the daytime the policeman himself, armed with a halberd, would appear at the door to salute with his inoffensive weapon the officers passing by, and would retire inside when dusk came, to employ himself either as a cobbler or in the manufacture of some special snuff patronised by the elder servants of the neighbourhood.

Life went on quietly and peacefully—at least for the outsider—in this Moscow Faubourg Saint-Germain. In the morning nobody was seen in the streets. About midday the children made their appearance under the

Princess Catherine Kropotkin.
(Mother of the author)

guidance of French tutors and German nurses, who took them out for a walk on the snow-covered boulevards. Later on in the day the ladies might be seen in their two-horse sledges, with a valet standing behind on a small plank fastened at the end of the runners, or ensconced in an old-fashioned carriage, immense and high, suspended on big curved springs and dragged by four horses, with a postillion in front and two valets standing behind. In the evening most of the houses were brightly illuminated, and, the blinds not being drawn down, the passer-by could admire the card-players or the waltzers in the saloons. ' Opinions ' were not in vogue in those days, and we were yet far from the years when in each one of these houses a struggle began between ' fathers and sons '—a struggle that usually ended either in a family tragedy or in a nocturnal visit of the state police. Fifty years ago nothing of the sort was thought of ; all was quiet and smooth—at least on the surface.

In this Old Equerries' Quarter I was born in 1842, and here I passed the first fifteen years of my life. Even after our father had sold the house in which our mother died, and bought another, and when again he had sold that house, and we spent several winters in hired houses, until he had found a third one to his taste within a stone's-throw of the church where he had been baptized, we still remained in the Old Equerries' Quarter, leaving it only during the summer to go to our country-seat.

II

A HIGH, spacious bedroom, the corner room of our house, with a wide bed upon which our mother is lying, our baby chairs and tables standing close by, and the neatly served tables covered with sweets and jellies in pretty glass jars—a room into which we children are ushered at a strange hour—this is the first half-distinct reminiscence of my life.

Our mother was dying of consumption; she was only thirty-five years old. Before parting with us for ever, she had wished to have us by her side, to caress us, to feel happy for a moment in our joys, and she had arranged this little treat by the side of her bed which she could leave no more. I remember her pale thin face, her large, dark brown eyes. She looked at us with love, and invited us to eat, to climb upon her bed ; then suddenly she burst into tears and began to cough, and we were told to go.

Some time after, we children—that is, my brother Alexander and myself—were removed from the big house to a small side house in the courtyard. The April sun filled the little rooms with its rays, but our German nurse Madame Búrman and Uliána, our Russian nurse, told us to go to bed. Their faces wet with tears, they were sewing for us black shirts fringed with broad white tassels. We could not sleep: the unknown frightened us, and we listened to their subdued talk. They said something about our mother which we could not understand. We jumped out of our beds, asking, ' Where is mamma ? Where is mamma ? '

Both of them burst into sobs, and began to pat our curly heads, calling us ' poor orphans,' until Uliána could hold out no longer, and said, ' Your mother is gone there—to the sky, to the angels.'

' How to the sky ? Why ? ' our infantile imagination in vain demanded.

This was in April 1846. I was only three and a half years old, and my brother Sásha not yet five. Where our elder brother and sister, Nicholas and Hélène, had gone I do not know : perhaps they were already at school. Nicholas was twelve years old, Hélène was eleven ; they kept together, and we knew them but little. So we remained, Alexander and I, in this little house, in the hands of Madame Búrman and Uliána. The good old German lady, homeless and absolutely alone in the wide world, took toward us the place of our mother. She brought us up as well as she could, buying us from time to time some simple toys, and overfeeding us with ginger cakes whenever another old German, who used to sell such cakes—probably as homeless and solitary as herself—paid an occasional visit to our house. We seldom saw our father, and the next two years passed without leaving any impression on my memory.

III

OUR father was very proud of the origin of his family, and would point with solemnity to a piece of parchment which hung on the wall of his study. It was decorated with our arms—the arms of the principality of Smolénsk covered with the ermine mantle and the crown of the Monomáchs—and there was written on it, and certified by the Heraldry Department, that our family originated with a grandson of Rostisláv Mstislávich the Bold (a name familiar in Russian history as that of a Grand Prince of Kíeff), and that our ancestors had been Grand Princes of Smolénsk.

'It cost me three hundred roubles to obtain that parchment,' our father used to say. .Like most people of his generation, he was not much versed in Russian history, and valued the parchment more for its cost than for its historical associations.

As a matter of fact, our family is of very ancient origin indeed ; but, like most descendants of Rurik who may be regarded as representative of the feudal period of Russian history, it was driven into the background when that period ended, and the Románoffs, enthroned at Moscow, began the work of consolidating the Russian state. In recent times, none of the Kropótkins seem to have had any special liking for state functions. Our great-grandfather and grandfather both retired from the military service when quite young men, and hastened to return to their family estates. It must also be said that of these estates the main one, Urúsovo, situated

in the government of Ryazán, on a high hill at the border
of fertile prairies, might tempt any one by the beauty of
its shadowy forests, its winding rivers, and its endless
meadows. Our grandfather was only a lieutenant when
he left the service, and retired to Urúsovo, devoting
himself to his estate, and to the purchase of other estates
in the neighbouring provinces.

Probably our generation would have done the same ;
but our grandfather married a Princess Gagárin, who
belonged to a quite different family. Her brother was
well known as a passionate lover of the stage. He kept
a private theatre of his own, and went so far in his
passion as to marry, to the scandal of all his relations,
a serf—the genial actress Semyónova, who was one of
the creators of dramatic art in Russia, and undoubtedly
one of its most sympathetic figures. To the horror of
' all Moscow,' she continued to appear on the stage.

I do not know if our grandmother had the same
artistic and literary tastes as her brother—I remember
her when she was already paralyzed and could speak only
in whispers ; but it is certain that in the next generation a leaning toward literature became a characteristic
of our family. One of the sons of the Princess Gagárin
was a minor Russian poet, and issued a book of poems
—a fact which my father was ashamed of and always
avoided mentioning ; and in our own generation several
of our cousins, as well as my brother and myself, have
contributed more or less to the literature of our period.

Our father was a typical officer of the time of
Nicholas I. Not that he was imbued with a warlike
spirit or much in love with camp life ; I doubt whether
he spent a single night of his life at a bivouac fire, or

took part in one battle. But under Nicholas I. that
was of quite secondary importance. The true military
man of those times was the officer who was enamoured
of the military uniform and utterly despised all other
sorts of attire ; whose soldiers were trained to perform
almost superhuman tricks with their legs and rifles (to
break the wood of the rifle into pieces while ' presenting
arms ' was one of those famous tricks) ; and who could
show on parade a row of soldiers as perfectly aligned and
as motionless as a row of toy-soldiers. ' Very good,'
the Grand Duke Mikhael said once of a regiment,
after having kept it for one hour presenting arms—
' only *they breathe* ! ' To respond to the then current
conception of a military man was certainly our father's
ideal.

True, he took part in the Turkish campaign of 1828 ;
but he managed to remain all the time on the staff of
the chief commander ; and if we children, taking advantage of a moment when he was in a particularly
good temper, asked him to tell us something about the
war, he had nothing to tell but of a fierce attack of
hundreds of Turkish dogs which one night assailed him
and his faithful servant, Frol, as they were riding with
despatches through an abandoned Turkish village. They
had to use swords to extricate themselves from the
hungry beasts. Bands of Turks would assuredly have
better satisfied our imagination, but we accepted the
dogs as a substitute. When, however, pressed by our
questions, our father told us how he had won the
cross of Saint Anne ' for gallantry,' and the golden
sword which he wore, I must confess we felt really
disappointed. His story was decidedly too prosaic.

The officers of the general staff were lodged in a Turkish village, when it took fire. In a moment the houses were enveloped in flames, and in one of them a child had been left behind. Its mother uttered despairing cries. Thereupon, Frol, who always accompanied his master, rushed into the flames and saved the child. The chief commander, who saw the act, at once gave father the cross for gallantry.

'But, father,' we exclaimed, 'it was Frol who saved the child!'

'What of that?' replied he, in the most naïve way. 'Was he not my man? It is all the same.'

He also took some part in the campaign of 1831, during the Polish Revolution, and in Warsaw he made the acquaintance of, and fell in love with, the youngest daughter of the commander of an army corps, General Sulíma. The marriage was celebrated with great pomp, in the Lazienki palace; the lieutenant-governor, Count Paskiévich, acting as nuptial godfather on the bridegroom's side. 'But your mother,' our father used to add, 'brought me no fortune whatever.'

Which was true. Her father, Nikolái Semyónovich Sulíma, was not versed in the art of making a career or a fortune. He must have had in him too much of the blood of those Cossacks of the Dnyéper, who knew how to fight the well-equipped, warlike Poles or armies of the Turks, three times more than themselves, but knew not how to avoid the snares of the Moscow diplomacy, and, after having fought against the Poles in the terrible insurrection of 1648, which was the beginning of the end for the Polish republic, lost all their liberties in falling under the dominion of the Russian Tsars. One

Sulíma was captured by the Poles and tortured to death
at Warsaw, but the other ' colonels ' of the same stock
only fought the more fiercely on that account, and
Poland lost Little Russia.   As to our grandfather, he
knew how, with his regiment of cuirassiers during
Napoleon I.'s invasion, to cut his way into a French
infantry square bristling with bayonets, and to recover,
after having been left for dead on the battle-field, with a
deep cut in his head; but he could not become a valet to
the favourite of Alexander I., the omnipotent Arakchéeff,
and was consequently sent into a sort of honorary exile,
first as a governor-general of West Siberia, and later of
East Siberia.   In those times such a position was considered more lucrative than a gold-mine, but our grandfather returned from Siberia as poor as he went, and left
only modest fortunes to his three sons and three daughters.   When I went to Siberia, in 1862, I often heard
his name mentioned with respect.   He was almost
driven to despair by the wholesale stealing which went
on in those provinces, and which he had no means to
repress.

Our mother was undoubtedly a remarkable woman
for the times she lived in.   Many years after her death
I discovered, in a corner of a storeroom of our country
house, a mass of papers covered with her firm but
pretty handwriting : diaries in which she wrote with
delight of the scenery of Germany, and spoke of her
sorrows and her thirst for happiness ; books which she
had filled with Russian verses prohibited by censorship —
among them the beautiful historical ballads of Ryléeff,
the poet, whom Nicholas I. hanged in 1826 ; other
books containing music, French dramas, verses of

Lamartine, and Byron's poems that she had copied ; and a great number of water-colour paintings.

Tall, slim, adorned with a mass of dark chestnut hair, with dark brown eyes and a tiny mouth, she looks quite lifelike in a portrait in oils that was painted *con amore* by a good artist. Always lively and often careless, she was fond of dancing, and the peasant women in our village would tell us how she would admire from a balcony their ring-dances—slow and full of grace—and how finally she would herself join in them. She had the nature of an artist. It was at a ball that she caught the cold that produced the inflammation of the lungs which brought her to the grave.

All who knew her loved her. The servants worshipped her memory. It was in her name that Madame Búrman took care of us, and in her name the Russian nurse bestowed upon us her love. While combing our hair, or signing us with the cross in our beds, Uliána would often say, 'And your mamma must now look upon you from the skies, and shed tears on seeing you, poor orphans.' Our whole childhood is irradiated by her memory. How often in some dark passage, the hand of a servant would touch Alexander or me with a caress ; or a peasant woman, on meeting us in the fields, would ask, 'Will you be as good as your mother was ? She took compassion on us. You will, surely.' 'Us' meant, of course, the serfs. I do not know what would have become of us if we had not found in our house, amidst the serf servants, that atmosphere of love which children must have around them. We were her children, we bore likeness to her, and they lavished their care upon us, sometimes in a touching form, as will be seen later on.

Men passionately desire to live after death, but they often pass away without noticing the fact that the memory of a really good person always lives. It is impressed upon the next generation, and is transmitted again to the children. Is not that an immortality worth striving for ?

IV

Two years after the death of our mother our father married again. He had already cast his eyes upon a nice-looking young person, this time belonging to a wealthy family, when the fates decided another way. One morning, while he was still in his dressing-gown, the servants rushed madly into his room, announcing the arrival of General Timoféeff, the commander of the sixth army corps, to which our father belonged. This favourite of Nicholas I. was a terrible man. He would order a soldier to be flogged almost to death for a mistake made during a parade, or he would degrade an officer and send him as a private to Siberia because he had met him in the street with the hooks on his high, stiff collar unfastened. With Nicholas General Timoféeff's word was all-powerful.

The general, who had never before been in our house, came to propose to our father to marry his wife's niece, Mademoiselle Elisabeth Karandinó, one of several daughters of an admiral of the Black Sea fleet

—a young lady with a classical Greek profile, said to have been very beautiful. Father accepted, and his second wedding, like the first, was solemnized with great pomp.

'You young people understand nothing of this kind of thing,' he said in conclusion, after having told me the story more than once, with a very fine humour which I will not attempt to reproduce. 'But do you know what it meant at that time, the commander of an army corps—above all, that one-eyed devil, as we used to call him—coming himself to propose? Of course she had no dowry; only a big trunk filled with ladies' finery, and that Martha, her one serf, dark as a gypsy, sitting upon it.'

I have no recollection whatever of this event. I only remember a big drawing-room in a richly furnished house, and in that room a young lady, attractive but with a rather too sharp southern look, gambolling with us, and saying, 'You see what a jolly mamma you will have;' to which Sásha and I, sulkily looking at her, replied, 'Our mamma has flown away to the sky.' We regarded so much liveliness with suspicion.

Winter came, and a new life began for us. Our house was sold and another was bought and furnished completely anew. All that could convey a reminiscence of our mother disappeared—her portraits, her paintings, her embroideries. In vain Madame Búrman implored to be retained in our house, and promised to devote herself to the baby our stepmother was expecting as to her own child: she was sent away. 'Nothing of the Sulímas in my house,' she was told. All connection with our uncles and aunts and our grandmother were broken. Uliána was married to Frol, who became a major-domo, while she was made housekeeper ; and for our education a richly paid French tutor, M. Poulain, and a miserably paid Russian student, N. P. Smirnóff, were engaged.

Many of the sons of the Moscow nobles were educated at that time by Frenchmen, who represented the débris of Napoleon's Grande Armée. M. Poulain was one of them. He had just finished the education of the youngest son of the novelist Zagóskin ; and his pupil, Serge, enjoyed in the Old Equerries' Quarter the reputation of being so well brought up that our father did not hesitate to engage M. Poulain for the considerable sum of six hundred roubles a year.

M. Poulain brought with him his setter, Trésor, his coffee-pot Napoléon, and his French text-books, and he began to rule over us and the serf Matvéi who was attached to our service.

His plan of education was very simple. After having woke us up he attended to his coffee, which he used to take in his room. While we were preparing the morning lessons he made his toilet with minute care : he shampooed his grey hair so as to conceal his growing baldness, put on his tail-coat, sprinkled and washed himself with eau-de-cologne, and then escorted us downstairs to say good-morning to our parents. We used to find our father and stepmother at breakfast, and on approaching them we recited in the most ceremonious manner, 'Bonjour, mon cher papa,' and 'Bonjour, ma chère maman,' and kissed their hands. M. Poulain made a very complicated and elegant obeisance in pronouncing the words, 'Bonjour, monsieur le prince,' and 'Bonjour, madame la princesse,' after which the procession immediately withdrew and retired upstairs. This ceremony was repeated every morning.

Then our work began. M. Poulain changed his tail-coat for a dressing-gown, covered his head with a leather cap, and dropping into an easy-chair said ' Recite the lesson.'

We recited it ' by heart ' from one mark which was made in the book with the nail to the next mark. M. Poulain had brought with him the grammar of Noël and Chapsal, memorable to more than one generation of Russian boys and girls ; a book of French dialogues ; a history of the world, in one volume ; and a universal geography, also in one volume. We had to commit to memory the grammar, the dialogues, the history, and the geography.

The grammar, with its well-known sentences, ' What is grammar ? ' ' The art of speaking and writing correctly,' went all right. But the history book, unfortunately, had a preface, which contained an enumeration of all the advantages which can be derived from a knowledge of history. Things went on smoothly enough with the first sentences. We recited : ' The prince finds in it magnanimous examples for governing his subjects ; the military commander learns from it the noble art of warfare.' But the moment we came to law all went wrong. ' The juris-consult meets in it '—but what the learned lawyer meets in history we never came to know That terrible word ' jurisconsult ' spoiled all the game. As soon as we reached it we stopped.

' On your knees, *gros pouff* ! ' exclaimed Poulain. (That was for me.) ' On your knees, *grand dada* ! '

(That was for my brother.)   And there we knelt, shedding tears and vainly endeavouring to learn all about the jurisconsult.

It cost us many pains, that preface ! We were already learning all about the Romans, and used to put our sticks in Uliána's scales when she was weighing rice, 'just like Brennus ; ' we jumped from our table and other precipices for the salvation of our country, in imitation of Curtius ; but M. Poulain would still from time to time return to the preface, and again put us on our knees for that very same jurisconsult. Was it strange that later on both my brother and I should entertain an undisguised contempt for jurisprudence ?

I do not know what would have happened with geography if M. Poulain's book had had a preface. But happily the first twenty pages of the book had been torn away (Serge Zagóskin, I suppose, rendered us that notable service), and so our lessons commenced with the twenty-first page, which began, ' of the rivers which water France.'

It must be confessed that things did not always end with kneeling. There was in the class-room a birch rod, and Poulain resorted to it when there was no hope of progress with the preface or with some dialogue on virtue and propriety ; but one day sister Hélène, who by this time had left the Catherine Institut des Demoiselles, and now occupied a room underneath ours, hearing our cries, rushed, all in tears, into our father's study, and bitterly reproached him with having handed us over to our stepmother, who had abandoned us to 'a retired French drummer.'   'Of course,' she cried, 'there is no one to take their part, but I cannot see my brothers being treated in this way by a drummer!'

Taken thus unprepared, our father could not make a stand. He began to scold Hélène, but ended by approving her devotion to her brothers. Thereafter the birch rod was reserved for teaching the rules of propriety to the setter, Trésor.

No sooner had M. Poulain discharged himself of his heavy educational duties than he became quite another man—a lively comrade instead of a gruesome teacher. After lunch he took us out for a walk, and there was no end to his tales: we chattered like birds. Though we never went with him beyond the first pages of syntax, we soon learned, nevertheless, 'to speak correctly;' we used to *think* in French; and when he had dictated to us half through a book of mythology, correcting our faults by the book, without ever trying to explain to us why a word must be written in a particular way, we had learned 'to write correctly.'

After dinner we had our lesson with the Russian teacher, a student of the faculty of law in the Moscow University. He taught us all 'Russian' subjects— grammar, arithmetic, history, and so on. But in those years serious teaching had not yet begun. In the meantime he dictated to us every day a page of history, and in that practical way we quickly learned to write Russian quite correctly.

Our best time was on Sundays, when all the family, with the exception of us children, went to dine with Madame la Générale Timoféeff. It would also happen occasionally that both M. Poulain and N. P. Smirnóff would be allowed to leave the house, and when this occurred we were placed under the care of Uliána. After a hurriedly eaten dinner we hastened to the great hall, to which the younger housemaids soon repaired. All sorts of games were started—blind man, vulture and chickens, and so on; and then, all of a sudden, Tíkhon, the Jack-of-all-trades, would appear with a violin. Dancing began; not that measured and tiresome dancing, under the direction of a French dancing-master ' on india-rubber legs,' which made part of our education, but free dancing which was not a lesson, and in which a score of couples turned round any way; and this was only preparatory to the still more animated and rather wild Cossack dance. Tíkhon would then hand the violin to one of the older men, and would begin to perform with his legs such wonderful feats that the doors leading to the hall would soon be filled by the cooks and even the coachmen, who came to see the dance so dear to the Russian heart.

About nine o'clock the big carriage was sent to fetch the family home. Tíkhon, brush in hand, crawled on the floor, to make it shine with its virgin glance, and perfect order was restored in the house. And if, next morning, we two had been submitted to the most severe cross-examination, not a word would have been dropped concerning the previous evening's amusements. We never would have betrayed any one of the servants, nor would they have betrayed us. One Sunday, my brother and I, playing alone in the wide hall, ran against a bracket which supported a costly lamp. The lamp was broken to pieces. Immediately a council was held by the servants. No one scolded us; but it was decided that early next morning Tíkhon should at his risk and peril slip out of the house and run to the Smiths' Bridge in order to buy another lamp of the same pattern. It cost fifteen roubles—an enormous sum for the servants; but it was done, and we never heard a word of reproach about it.

When I think of it now, and all these scenes come back to my memory, I notice that we never heard coarse language in any of the games, nor saw in the dances anything like the kind of dancing which children are now taken to admire in the theatres. In the servants' house, among themselves, they assuredly used coarse expressions; but we were children—*her* children —and that protected us from anything of the sort.

In those days children were not bewildered by a profusion of toys, as they are now. We had almost none, and were thus compelled to rely upon our own inventiveness. Besides, we both had early acquired a taste for the theatre. The inferior carnival theatres, with the thieving and fighting shows, produced no lasting impression upon us: we ourselves played enough at robbers and soldiers. But the great star of the ballet, Fanny Elssler, came to Moscow, and we saw her. When father took a box in the theatre, he always secured one of the best, and paid for it well; but then he insisted that all the members of the family should enjoy it to its full value. Small though I was at that time, Fanny Elssler left upon me the impression of a being so full of grace, so light, and so artistic in all her movements, that ever since I have been unable to feel the slightest interest in a dance which belongs more to the domain of gymnastics than to the domain of art.

Of course the ballet that we saw—'Gitana,' the Spanish Gypsy—had to be repeated at home ; its substance, not the dances. We had a ready-made stage, as the doorway which led from our bedroom into the class-room had a curtain instead of a door. A few chairs put in a half-circle in front of the curtain, with an easy-chair for M. Poulain, became the hall and the imperial box, and an audience could easily be mustered with the Russian teacher, Uliána, and a couple of maids from the servants' rooms.

Two scenes of the ballet had to be represented by some means or other : the one where the little Gitana is brought by the gypsies into their camp in a wheel-barrow, and that in which Gitana makes her first appearance on the stage, descending from a hill and crossing a bridge over a brook which reflects her image. The audience burst into frantic applause at this point, and the cheers were evidently called forth—so we thought, at least—by the reflection in the brook.

We found our Gitana in one of the youngest girls in the maid-servants' room. Her rather shabby blue cotton dress was no obstacle to personifying Fanny Elssler. An overturned chair, pushed along by its legs, head downwards, was an acceptable substitute for the wheelbarrow. But the brook ! Two chairs and the long ironing-board of Andréi, the tailor, made the bridge, and a piece of blue cotton made the brook. The image in the brook, however, would not appear full size, do what we might with M. Poulain's little shaving-glass. After many unsuccessful endeavours we had to give it up, but we bribed Uliána to behave as if she saw the image, and to applaud loudly at this passage, so that finally we began to believe that perhaps something of it could be seen.

Racine's 'Phèdre,' or at least the last act of it, also went off nicely; that is, Sásha recited the melodious verses beautifully—

A peine nous sortions des portes de Trézène;

and I sat absolutely motionless and unconcerned during the whole length of the tragic monologue intended to apprise me of the death of my son, down to the place where, according to the book, I had to exclaim, 'O dieux!'

But whatsoever we might impersonate, all our performances invariably ended with hell. All candles save one were put out, and this one was placed behind a transparent paper to imitate flames, while my brother and I, concealed from view, howled in the most appalling way as the condemned. Uliána, who did not like to have any allusion to the evil one made at bedtime, looked horrified; but I ask myself now whether this extremely concrete representation of hell, with a candle and a sheet of paper, did not contribute to free us both at an early age from the fear of eternal fire. Our conception of it was too realistic to resist scepticism.

I must have been very much of a child when I saw the great Moscow actors: Schépkin, Sadóvskiy, and Shúmski, in Gogol's *Revisór* and another comedy; still, I remember not only the salient scenes of the two plays, but even the attitudes and expressions of these great actors of the realistic school which is now so admirably represented by Duse. I remembered them so well that when I saw the same plays given at St. Petersburg by actors belonging to the French declamatory school, I found no pleasure in their acting, always comparing them with Schépkin and Sadóvskiy, by whom my taste in dramatic art was settled.

This makes me think that parents who wish to develop artistic taste in their children ought to take them occasionally to really well-acted, good plays, instead of feeding them on a profusion of so-called ' children's pantomimes.'

V

WHEN I was in my eighth year, the next step in my career was taken, in a quite unforeseen way. I do not know exactly on what occasion it happened, but probably it was on the twenty-fifth anniversary of Nicholas I.'s reign, when great festivities were arranged at Moscow. The imperial family were coming to the old capital, and the Moscow nobility intended to celebrate this event by a fancy-dress ball in which children were to play an important part. It was agreed that the whole motley crowd of nationalities of which the population of the Russian Empire is composed should be represented at this ball to greet the monarch. Great preparations went on in our house, as well as in all the houses of our neighbourhood.

Some sort of remarkable Russian costume was made for our stepmother. Our father, being a military man, had to appear, of course, in his uniform; but those of our relatives who were not in the military service were as busy with their Russian, Greek, Caucasian, and Mongolian costumes, as the ladies themselves. When the Moscow nobility gives a ball to the imperial family, it must be something extraordinary. As for my brother Alexander and myself, we were considered too young to take part in so important a ceremonial.

And yet, after all, I did take part in it. Our mother was an intimate friend of Madame Nazímoff, the wife of the general who was Governor of Wilno when the emancipation of the serfs began to be spoken of. Madame Nazímoff, who was a very beautiful woman, was expected to be present at the ball with her child, about ten years old, and to wear some wonderful costume of a Persian princess in harmony with which the costume of a young Persian prince, exceedingly rich, with a belt covered with jewels, was made ready for her son. But the boy fell ill just before the ball, and Madame Nazímoff thought that one of the children of her best friend would be a good substitute for her own child. Alexander and I were taken to her house to try on the costume. It proved to be too short for Alexander, who was much taller than I, but it fitted me exactly, and therefore it was decided that I should impersonate the Persian prince.

The immense hall of the House of the Moscow nobility was crowded with guests. Each of the children received a standard bearing at its top the arms of one of the sixty provinces of the Russian Empire. I had an eagle floating over a blue sea, which represented, as I learned later on, the arms of the government of Astrakhan, on the Caspian Sea. We were then ranged at the back of the great hall, and slowly marched in two rows toward the raised platform upon which the Emperor and his family stood. As we reached it we went right and left, and thus stood aligned in one row before the platform. At a given signal all standards were lowered before the Emperor. The apotheosis of autocracy was made most impressive: Nicholas was enchanted. All provinces of the Empire worshipped the supreme ruler. Then we children slowly retired to the rear of the hall.

But here some confusion occurred. Chamberlains in their gold-embroidered uniforms were running about, and I was taken out of the ranks; my uncle, Prince Gagárin, dressed as a Tungus (I was dizzy with admiration of his fine leather coat, his bow, and his quiver full of arrows), lifted me up in his arms, and planted me on the imperial platform.

Whether it was because I was the tiniest in the row of boys, or that my round face, framed in curls, looked funny under the high Astrakhan fur bonnet I wore, I know not, but Nicholas wanted to have me on the platform; and there I stood amidst generals and ladies looking down upon me with curiosity. I was told later on that Nicholas I., who was always fond of barrack jokes, took me by the arm, and, leading me to Marie Alexándrovna (the wife of the heir to the throne), who was then expecting her third child, said in his military way, 'That is the sort of boy you must bring me'—a joke which made her blush deeply. I well remember, at any rate, Nicholas asking me whether I would have sweets; but I replied that I should like to have some of those tiny biscuits which were served with tea (we were never overfed at home), and he called a waiter and emptied a full tray into my tall bonnet. 'I will take them to Sásha,' I said to him.

However, the soldier-like brother of Nicholas, Mikhael, who had the reputation of being a wit, managed to make me cry. 'When you are a good boy,' he said, 'they treat you so,' and he passed his big hand over my face downwards; 'but when you are naughty, they treat you so,' and he passed the hand upwards, rubbing my nose, which already had a marked tendency toward growing in that direction. Tears, which I vainly tried to stop, came into my eyes. The ladies at once took my part, and the good-hearted Marie Alexándrovna took me under her protection. She set me by her side, in a high velvet chair with a gilded back, and our people told me afterward that I very soon put my head in her lap and went to sleep. She did not leave her chair during the whole time the ball was going on.

I remember also that, as we were waiting in the entrance-hall for our carriage, our relatives petted and kissed me, saying, 'Pétya, you have been made a page;' but I answered, 'I am not a page; I will go home,' and was very anxious about my bonnet which contained the pretty little biscuits that I was taking home for Sásha.

I do not know whether Sásha got many of those biscuits, but I recollect what a hug he gave me when he was told about my anxiety concerning the bonnet.

To be inscribed as a candidate for the corps of pages was then a great favour, which Nicholas seldom bestowed on the Moscow nobility. My father was delighted, and already dreamed of a brilliant court career for his son. Our stepmother, every time she told the story, never failed to add, 'It is all because I gave him my blessing before he went to the ball.'

Madame Nazímoff was delighted, too, and insisted upon having her portrait painted in the costume in which she looked so beautiful, with me standing at her side.

My brother Alexander's fate, also, was decided next year. The jubilee of the Izmáylovsk regiment, to which my father had belonged in his youth, was celebrated about this time at St. Petersburg. One night, while all the household was plunged in deep sleep, a three-horse carriage, ringing with the bells attached to the harnesses, stopped at our gate. A man jumped out of it, loudly shouting, 'Open ! An ordinance from his Majesty the Emperor.'

One can easily imagine the terror which this nocturnal visit spread in our house. My father, trembling, went down to his study. 'Court-martial, degradation as a soldier,' were words which rang then in the ears of every military man ; it was a terrible epoch. But Nicholas simply wanted to have the names of the sons of all the officers who had once belonged to the regiment, in order to send the boys to military schools, if that had not yet been done. A special messenger had been dispatched for that purpose from St. Petersburg to Moscow, and now he called day and night at the houses of the ex-Izmáylovsk officers.

With a shaking hand my father wrote that his eldest son, Nicholas, was already in the first corps of cadets at Moscow ; that his youngest son, Peter, was a candidate for the corps of pages; and that there remained only his second son, Alexander, who had not yet entered the military career. A few weeks later came a paper informing father of the 'monarch's favour.' Alexander was ordered to enter a corps of cadets in Orel, a small provincial town. It cost my father a deal of trouble and a large sum of money to get Alexander sent to a corps of cadets at Moscow. This new 'favour ' was obtained only in consideration of the fact that our elder brother was in that corps.

And thus, owing to the will of Nicholas I., we had both to receive a military education, though, before we were many years older, we simply hated the military career for its absurdity. But Nicholas I. was watchful that none of the sons of the nobility should embrace any other profession than the military one, unless they were of infirm health ; and so we had all three to be officers, to the great satisfaction of my father.

VI

WEALTH was measured in those times by the number of ' souls ' which a landed proprietor owned. So many ' souls ' meant so many male serfs : women did not

count.   My father, who owned nearly twelve hundred
souls, in three different provinces, and who had, in
addition to his peasants' holdings, large tracts of land
which were cultivated by these peasants, was accounted
a rich man.   He lived up to his reputation, which
meant that his house was open to any number of
visitors, and that he kept a very large household.

We were a family of eight, occasionally of ten or
twelve ; but fifty servants at Moscow, and half as many
more in the country, were considered not one too
many.   Four coachmen to attend a dozen horses, three
cooks for the masters and two more for the servants, a
dozen men to wait upon us at dinner-time (one man,
plate in hand, standing behind each person seated at the
table), and girls innumerable in the maid-servants' room,
—how could anyone do with less than this ?

Besides, the ambition of every landed proprietor
was that everything required for his household should
be made at home by his own men.

'How nicely your piano is always tuned !   I suppose
Herr Schimmel must be your tuner ? ' perhaps a visitor
would remark.

To be able to answer, 'I have my own piano-tuner,'
was in those times the correct thing.

'What beautiful pastry ! ' the guests would exclaim,
when a work of art, composed of ices and pastry,
appeared toward the end of the dinner.   'Confess,
prince, that it comes from Tremblé' (the fashionable
pastry-cook).

'It is made by my own confectioner, a pupil of
Tremblé, whom I have allowed to show what he can
do,' was a reply which elicited general admiration.

To have embroideries, harnesses, furniture—in fact, everything—made by one's own men was the ideal of the rich and respected landed proprietor. As soon as the children of the servants attained the age of ten, they were sent as apprentices to the fashionable shops, where they were obliged to spend five or seven years chiefly in sweeping, in receiving an incredible number of thrashings, and in running about town on errands of all sort. I must own that few of them became masters of their respective arts. The tailors and the shoe-makers were found only skilful enough to make clothes or shoes for the servants, and when a really good pastry was required for a dinner-party it was ordered at Tremblé's, while our own confectioner was beating the drum in the music band.

That band was another of my father's ambitions, and almost every one of his male servants, in addition to other accomplishments, was a bass-viol or a clarinet in the band. Makár, the piano-tuner, *alias* under-butler, was also a flutist ; Andréi, the tailor, played the French horn ; the confectioner was first put to beat the drum, but he misused his instrument to such a deafening degree that a tremendous trumpet was bought for him, in the hope that his lungs would not have the power to make the same noise as his hands ; when, however, this last hope had to be abandoned, he was sent to be a soldier. As to 'spotted Tíkhon,' in addition to his numerous functions in the household as lamp-cleaner, floor-polisher, and footman, he made himself useful in the band—to-day as a trombone, to-morrow as a bassoon, and occasionally as second violin.

The two first violins were the only exceptions to the

rule : they were ' violins,' and nothing else. My father had bought them, with their large families, for a handsome sum of money, from his sisters (he never bought serfs from nor sold them to strangers). In the evenings when he was not at his club, or when there was a dinner or an evening party at our house, the band of twelve to fifteen musicians was summoned. They played very nicely, and were in great demand for dancing-parties in the neighbourhood; still more when we were in the country. This was, of course, a constant source of gratification to my father, whose permission had to be asked to get the assistance of his band.

Nothing, indeed, gave him more pleasure than to be asked for help, either in the way mentioned or in any other : for instance, to obtain free education for a boy, or to save somebody from a punishment inflicted upon him by a law court. Although he was liable to fall into fits of rage, he was undoubtedly possessed of a natural instinct toward leniency, and when his patronage was requested he would write scores of letters in all possible directions, to all sorts of persons of high standing, in favour of his protégé. At such times, his mail, which was always heavy, would be swollen by half a dozen special letters, written in a most original, semi-official, and semi-humorous style ; each of them sealed, of course, with his arms, in a big square envelope, which rattled like a baby-rattle on account of the quantity of sand it contained—the use of blotting-paper being then unknown. The more difficult the case, the more energy he would display, until he secured the favour he asked for his protégé, whom in many cases he never saw.

My father liked to have plenty of guests in his house. Our dinner-hour was four, and at seven the family gathered round the *samovár* (tea-urn) for tea. Everyone belonging to our circle could drop in at that hour, and from the time my sister Hélène was again with us' there was no lack of visitors, old and young, who took advantage of the privilege. When the windows facing the street showed bright light inside that was enough to let people know that the family was at home and friends would be welcome.

Nearly every night we had visitors. The green tables were opened in the hall for the card-players, while the ladies and the young people stayed in the reception-room or around Hélène's piano. When the ladies had gone, card-playing continued sometimes till the small hours of the morning, and considerable sums of money changed. hands among the players. Father invariably lost. But the real danger for him was not at home : it was at the English Club, where the stakes were much higher than in private houses, and especially when he was induced to join a party of ' very respectable ' gentlemen, in one of the aristocratic houses of the Old Equerries' Quarter, where gambling went on all night. On an occasion of this kind his losses were sure to be heavy.

Dancing-parties were not infrequent, to say nothing of a couple of obligatory balls every winter. Father's way, in such cases, was to have everything done in a good style, whatever the expense. But at the same time such niggardliness was practised in our house in daily life that if I were to recount it, I should be accused of exaggeration. It is said of a family of pretenders

to the throne of France, renowned for their truly regal
hunting-parties, that in their everyday life even the
tallow candles are minutely counted. The same sort
of miserly economy ruled in our house with regard to
everything ; so much so that when we, the children of the
house, grew up, we detested all saving and counting.
However, in the Old Equerries' Quarter such a mode of
life only raised my father in public esteem. ' The old
prince,' it was said, ' seems to be sharp over money
at home ; but he knows how a nobleman ought to
live.'

In our quiet and clean lanes that was the kind of
life which was most in respect. One of our neighbours,
General D——, kept his house up in very grand style ;
and yet the most comical scenes took place every
morning between him and his cook. Breakfast over,
the old general, smoking his pipe, would himself order
the dinner.

' Well, my boy,' he would say to the cook, who
appeared in snow-white attire, ' to-day we shall not be
many : only a couple of guests. You will make us a
soup, you know, with some spring delicacies—green
peas, French beans, and so on. You have not given us
any yet, and madam, you know, likes a good French
spring soup.'

' Yes, sir.'

' Then, anything you like as an entrée.'

' Yes, sir.'

' Of course, asparagus is not yet in season, but I saw
yesterday such nice bundles of it in the shops.'

' Yes, sir ; eight shillings the bundle.'

' Quite right ! Then, we are sick of your roasted

chickens and turkeys ; you ought to get something for a change.'

' Some venison, sir ? '

' Yes, yes, anything for a change.'

And when the six courses of dinner had been decided on, the old general would ask, ' Now how much shall I give you for to-day's expenses ?   Six shillings will do, I suppose ? '

' One pound, sir.'

' What nonsense, my boy !   Here are six shillings ; I assure you that's quite enough.'

' Eight shillings for asparagus, five for the vegetables.'

' Now, look here, my dear boy, be reasonable.   I'll go as high as seven-and-six, and you must be economical.'

And the bargaining would go on thus for half an hour, until the two would agree upon fourteen shillings and sixpence, with the understanding that the morrow's dinner should not cost more than three shillings. Whereupon the general, quite happy at having made such a good bargain, would take his sledge, make a round of the fashionable shops, and return quite radiant, bringing for his wife a bottle of exquisite perfume, for which he had paid a fancy price in a French shop, and announcing to his only daughter that a new velvet mantle—' something very simple '. and very costly— would be sent for her to try on that afternoon.

All our relatives, who were numerous on my father's side, lived exactly in the same way : and if a new spirit occasionally made its appearance, it usually took the form of some religious passion.   Thus a Prince Gagárin joined the Jesuit order, again to the scandal of ' all

Moscow,' another young prince entered a monastery, while several older ladies became fanatic devotees.

There was a single exception. One of our nearest relatives, Prince—let me call him Mírski—had spent his youth at St. Petersburg as an officer of the Guards. He took no interest in keeping his own tailors and cabinet-makers, for his house was furnished in a grand modern style, and his wearing apparel was all made in the best St. Petersburg shops. Gambling was not his propensity—he played cards only when in company with ladies ; but his weak point was his dinner-table, upon which he spent incredible sums of money.

Lent and Easter were his chief epochs of extravagance. When the Great Lent came, and it would not have been proper to eat meat, cream, or butter, he seized the opportunity to invent all sorts of delicacies in the way of fish. The best shops of the two capitals were ransacked for that purpose ; special emissaries were dispatched from his estate to the mouth of the Vólga, to bring back on post-horses (there was no railway at that time) a sturgeon of great size or some extraordinarily cured fish. And when Easter came, there was no end to his inventions.

Easter, in Russia, is the most venerated and also the gayest of the yearly festivals. It is the festival of spring. The immense heaps of snow which have been lying during the winter along the streets rapidly thaw, and roaring streams run down the streets ; not like a thief who creeps in by insensible degrees, but frankly and openly spring comes—every day bringing with it a change in the state of the snow and the progress of the buds on the trees ; the night frosts only keep the thaw within reasonable bounds. The last week of the Great Lent, Passion Week, was kept in Moscow, in my childhood, with extreme solemnity; it was a time of general mourning, and crowds of people went to the churches to listen to the impressive reading of those passages of the Gospels which relate the sufferings of the Christ. Not only were meat, eggs, and butter not eaten, but even fish was refused; some of the most rigorous taking no food at all on Good Friday. The more striking was the contrast when Easter came.

On Saturday everyone attended the night service which began in a mournful way. Then, suddenly, at midnight, the resurrection news was announced. All the churches were at once illuminated, and gay peals of bells resounded from hundreds of bell towers. General rejoicing began. All the people kissed one another thrice on the cheeks, repeating the resurrection words, and the churches, now flooded with light, shone with the gay toilettes of the ladies. The poorest woman had a new dress; if she had only one new dress a year, she would get it for that night.

At the same time, Easter was, and is still, the signal for a real debauch in eating. Special Easter cream cheeses (*páskha*) and Easter bread (*koolích*) are prepared; and everyone, no matter how poor he or she may be, must have a small páskha and a small koolích, with at least one egg painted red, to be consecrated in the church, and to be used afterward to break the Lent. With most old Russians, eating began at night, after a short Easter mass, immediately after the consecrated food had been brought from church; but in the houses of the nobility the ceremony was postponed till Sunday

morning, when a table was covered with all sorts of
viands, cheeses, and pastry, and all the servants came
to exchange with their masters three kisses and a red-
painted egg.   Throughout Easter week a table spread
with Easter food stood in the great hall, and every
visitor was invited to partake.

On this occasion Prince Mírski surpassed himself.
Whether he was at St. Petersburg or at Moscow,
messengers brought to his house, from his estate, a
specially prepared cream cheese for the páskha, and
his cook managed to make out of it a piece of artistic
confectionery.   Other messengers were dispatched to
the province of Nóvgorod to get a bear's ham, which
was cured for the prince's Easter table.   And while
the princess, with her two daughters, visited the most
austere monasteries, in which the night service would
last three or four hours in succession, and spent all
Passion Week in the most mournful condition of mind,
eating only a piece of dry bread between the visits she
paid to Russian, Roman, and Protestant preachers, her
husband made every morning the tour of the well-
known Milútin shops at St. Petersburg, where all
possible delicacies are brought from the ends of the
earth.   There he used to select the most extravagant
dainties for his Easter table.   Hundreds of visitors
came to his house, and were asked ' just to taste ' this
or that extraordinary thing.

The end of it was that the prince managed literally
to eat up a considerable fortune.   His richly furnished
house and beautiful estate were sold, and when he and
his wife were old they had nothing left, not even a
home, and were compelled to live with their children.

No wonder that when the emancipation of the serfs came, nearly all these families of the Old Equerries' Quarter were ruined. But I must not anticipate events.

VII

To maintain such numbers of servants as were kept in our house would have been ruinous if all provisions had to be bought at Moscow; but in those times of serfdom things were managed very simply. When winter came, father sat at his table and wrote the following :—

'To the manager of my estate, Nikólskoye, situated in the government of Kalúga, district of Meschóvsk, on the river Siréna, from the Prince Alexéi Petróvich Kropótkin, Colonel and Commander of various orders.

'On receipt of this, and as soon as winter communication is established, thou art ordered to send to my house, situated in the city of Moscow, twenty-five peasant-sledges, drawn by two horses each, one horse from each house, and one sledge and one man from each second house, and to load them with [so many] quarters of oats, [so many] of wheat, and [so many] of rye, as also with all the poultry and geese and ducks, well frozen, which have to be killed this winter, well packed and accompanied by a complete list, under the supervision of a well-chosen man ; ' and so it went on for a couple of pages, till the next full-stop was reached. After this there followed an enumeration of the penalties which would be inflicted in case the provisions should not reach the house situated in such a street, number so-and-so, in due time and in good condition.

Some time before Christmas the twenty-five peasant-sledges really entered our gates, and covered the surface of the wide yard.

'Frol!' shouted my father, as soon as the report of this great event reached him.   'Kiryúshka! Yegórka! Where are they?   Everything will be stolen!   Frol, go and receive the oats!   Uliána, go and receive the poultry! Kiryúshka, call the princess!'

All the household was in commotion, the servants running wildly in every direction, from the hall to the yard, and from the yard to the hall, but chiefly to the maid-servants' room, to communicate there the Nikólskoye news : 'Pásha is going to marry after Christmas.   Aunt Anna has surrendered her soul to God,' and so on.   Letters had also come from the country, and very soon one of the maids would steal upstairs into my room.

'Are you alone?   The teacher is not in ? '

' No, he is at the university.'

' Well, then, be kind and read me this letter from mother.'

And I would read to her the naïve letter, which always began with the words, ' Father and mother send you their blessing for ages not to be broken.'   After this came the news : ' Aunt Eupraxie lies ill, all her bones aching ; and your cousin is not yet married, but hopes to be after Easter ; and aunt Stepanída's cow died on All Saints' day.' Following the news came the greetings, two pages of them : ' Brother Paul sends you his greetings, and the sisters Mary and Dária send their greetings, and then uncle Dmítri sends his many greetings,' and so on. However, notwithstanding the monotomy of the enumeration, each name awakened some remarks : 'Then she is still alive, poor soul, if she sends her greetings ; it is nine years since she has lain motionless.' Or, 'Oh, he has not forgotten me; he must be back, then, for Christmas; such a nice boy. You will write me a letter, won't you ? and I must not forget him then.' I promised, of course, and when the time came I wrote a letter in exactly the same style.

When the sledges had been unloaded, the hall filled with peasants. They had put on their best coats over their sheepskins, and waited until father should call them into his room to have a talk about the snow and the prospects of the next crops. They hardly dared to walk in their heavy boots on the polished floor. A few ventured to sit down on the edge of an oak bench; they emphatically refused to make use of chairs. So they waited for hours, looking with alarm upon everyone who entered father's room or issued from it.

Some time later on, usually next morning, one of the servants would run slyly upstairs to the class-room.

'Are you alone ? '

'Yes.'

'Then go quickly to the hall. The peasants want to see you; something from your nurse.'

When I went down to the hall, one of the peasants would give me a little bundle containing perhaps a few rye cakes, half a dozen hard-boiled eggs, and some apples, tied in a motley coloured cotton kerchief.

' Take that : it is your nurse, Vasilísa, who sends it to
you. Look if the apples are not frozen. I hope not :
I kept them all the journey on my breast. Such a
fearful frost we had.' And the broad, bearded face,
covered with frost-bites, would smile radiantly, showing
two rows of beautiful white teeth from beneath quite a
forest of hair.

'And this is for your brother, from his nurse Anna,'
another peasant would say, handing me a similar bundle.
' " Poor boy," she says, " he can never have enough at
school." '

Blushing and not knowing what to say, I would
murmur at last, ' Tell Vasilísa that I kiss her, and Anna
too, for my brother.' At which all faces would become
still more radiant.

' Yes, I will, to be sure.'

Then Kiríla, who kept watch at father's door,
would whisper suddenly, ' Run quickly upstairs ; your
father may come out in a moment. Don't forget the
kerchief ; they want to take it back.'

As I carefully folded the worn kerchief, I most
passionately desired to send Vasilísa something. But I
had nothing to send, not even a toy, and we never had
pocket-money.

Our best time, of course, was in the country. As
soon as Easter and Whitsuntide had passed, all our
thoughts were directed towards Nikólskoye. However,
time went on—the lilacs must be past blooming at
Nikólskoye—and father had still thousands of affairs
to keep him in town. At last, five or six peasant-carts
entered our yard : they came to take all sorts of things

which had to be sent to the country house. The great
old coach and the other coaches in which we were
going to make the journey were taken out and
inspected once more. The boxes began to be packed.
Our lessons made slow progress; at every moment we
interrupted our teachers, asking whether this or that
book should be taken with us, and long before all
others we began packing our books, our slates, and our
toys, which were of our own making.

Everything was ready : the peasant-carts stood
heavily loaded with furniture for the country house,
boxes containing the kitchen utensils, and almost
countless empty glass jars which were to be brought
back in the autumn filled with all kinds of preserves.
The peasants waited every morning for hours in the
hall; but the order for leaving did not come. Father
continued to write all the morning in his room, and
disappeared at night. Finally, our stepmother interfered, her maid having ventured to report that the
peasants were very anxious to return, as haymaking
was near.

Next afternoon, Frol, the major-domo, and Mikhael
Aléeff, the first violin, were called into father's room. A
sack containing the ' food money '—that is, a few coppers
a day—for each of the forty or fifty souls who were to
accompany the household to Nikólskoye, was handed
to Frol, with a list. All were enumerated in that list :
the band in full; then the cooks and the under-cooks,
the laundresses, the under-laundress, who was blessed
with a family of six mites, ' Polka Squinting,' ' Domna
the Big One,' ' Domna the Small One,' and the rest
of them.

The first violin received an 'order of march.' I knew it well, because father, seeing that he never would be ready, had called me to copy it into the book, in which he used to copy all 'outgoing papers':—

'To my house servant, Mikhael Aléeff, from Prince Alexéi Petróvich Kropótkin, Colonel and Commander.

'Thou art ordered, on May 29, at six A.M., to march out with my loads, from the city of Moscow, for my estate, situated in the government of Kalúga, district of Meschóvsk, on the river Siréna, representing a distance of one hundred and sixty miles from this house; to look after the good conduct of the men entrusted to thee, and if any one of them proves to be guilty of misconduct, or of drunkenness, or of insubordination, to bring the said man before the commander of the garrison detachment of the separate corps of the interior garrisons, with the inclosed circular letter, and to ask that he may be punished by flogging [the first violin knew who was meant], as an example to the others.

'Thou art ordered, moreover, to look especially after the integrity of the goods entrusted to thy care, and to march according to the following order: First day, stay at village So-and-So, to feed the horses; second day, spend the night at the town of Podólsk;' and so on for all the seven or eight days that the journey would last.

Next day, at ten instead of at six—punctuality is not a Russian virtue ('Thank God, we are not Germans,' true Russians used to say), the carts left the house. The servants had to make the journey on foot; only the children were accommodated with a seat in a bath-

tub or basket, on the top of a loaded cart, and some of
the women might find an occasional resting-place on the
ledge of a cart. The others had to walk all the hundred
and sixty miles. As long as they were marching
through Moscow, discipline was maintained : it was
peremptorily forbidden to wear top-boots or to pass a
belt over the coat. But when they were on the road,
and we overtook them a couple of days later, and
especially when it was known that father would stay a
few days longer at Moscow, the men and the women—
dressed in all sorts of impossible coats, belted with
cotton handkerchiefs, burned by the sun or dripping
under the rain, and helping themselves along with
sticks cut in the woods—certainly looked more like a
wandering band of gypsies than the household of a
wealthy landowner. Similar peregrinations were made
by every household in those times, and when we saw a
file of servants marching along one of our streets, we
at once knew that the Apúkhtins or the Pryánishnikoffs
were migrating.

The carts were gone, yet the family did not move.
All of us were sick of waiting ; but father still continued to write interminable orders to the managers of
his estates, and I copied them diligently into the big
'outgoing book.' At last the order to start was given.
We were called downstairs. My father read aloud the
order of march, addressed to 'the Princess Kropótkin,
wife of Prince Alexéi Petróvich Kropótkin, Colonel and
Commander,' in which the halting-places during the
five days' journey were duly enumerated. True, the
order was written for May 30, and the departure was
fixed for nine A.M., though May was gone, and the

departure took place in the afternoon : this upset all
calculations.   But, as is usual in military marching-
orders, this circumstance had been foreseen, and was
provided for in the following paragraph :—

'If, however, contrary to expectation, the departure of your highness does not take place at the said
day and hour, you are requested to act according to
the best of your understanding, in order to bring the
said journey to its best issue.'

Then, all present, the family and the servants, sat
down for a moment, signed themselves with the cross,
and bade my father good-bye.   'I entreat you, Alexis,
don't go to the club,' our stepmother whispered to him.
The great coach, drawn by four horses, with a postilion,
stood at the door, with its little folding ladder to
facilitate climbing in ; the other coaches also were
there.   Our seats were enumerated in the marching-
orders, but our stepmother had to exercise 'the best of
her understanding' even at that early stage of the
proceedings, and we started to the great satisfaction
of all.

The journey was an inexhaustible source of enjoyment for us children.   The stages were short, and we
stopped twice a day to feed the horses.   As the ladies
screamed at the slightest declivity of the road, it was
found more convenient to alight each time the road
went up or down hill, which it did continually, and we
took advantage of this to have a peep into the woods
by the roadside, or a run along some crystal brook.
The beautifully kept high road from Moscow to Warsaw,
which we followed for some distance, was covered,
moreover, with a variety of interesting objects : files of

loaded carts, groups of pilgrims, and all sorts of people. Twice a day we stopped in large, animated villages, and after a good deal of bargaining about the prices to be charged for hay and oats, as well as for the samovárs, we dismounted at the gates of an inn. Cook Andréi bought a, chicken and made the soup, while we ran in the meantime to the next wood, or examined the farm-yard, the gardens, the inner life of the inn.

At Máloyaroslávetz, where a battle was fought in 1812, when the Russian army vainly attempted to stop Napoleon in his retreat from Moscow, we usually spent the night. M. Poulain, who had been wounded in the Spanish campaign, knew, or pretended to know, every-thing about the battle at Máloyaroslávetz. He took us to the battlefield, and explained how the Russians tried to check Napoleon's advance, and how the Grande Armée crushed them and made its way through the Russian lines. He explained it as well as if he himself had taken part in the battle. Here the Cossacks attempted *un mouvement tournant*, but Davout, or some other marshal, routed them and pursued them just beyond these hills on the right. There the left wing of Napoleon crushed the Russian infantry, and here Napoleon himself, at the head of the Old Guard, charged Kutúzoff's centre, and covered himself and his Guard with undying glory.

We once took the old Kalúga route, and stopped at Tarútino ; but here M. Poulain was much less eloquent. For it was at this place that Napoleon, who intended to retreat by a southern route, was compelled, after a bloody battle, to abandon his plan, and was forced to take the Smolénsk route, which his army had laid waste during its march on Moscow. However, in M. Poulain's narrative, Napoleon did not lose the battle : he was only deceived by his marshals; otherwise he would have marched straight upon Kíeff and Odéssa, and his eagles would have floated over the Black Sea.

Beyond Kalúga we had to cross for a stretch of five miles a beautiful pine forest, which remains connected in my memory with some of the happiest reminiscences of my childhood. The sand in that forest was as deep as in an African desert, and we went all the way on foot, while the horses, stopping every moment, slowly dragged the carriages in the sand. When I was in my teens, it was my delight to leave the family behind, and to walk the whole distance by myself. Immense red pines, centuries old, rose on every side, and not a sound reached the ear except the voices of the lofty trees. In a small ravine a fresh crystal spring murmured, and a passer-by had left in it, for the use of those who should come after him, a small funnel-shaped ladle, made of birch bark, with a split stick for a handle. Noiselessly a squirrel ran up a tree, and the underwood was as full of mysteries as were the trees. In that forest my first love of Nature and my first dim perception of its incessant life were born.

Beyond the forest, and past the ferry which took us over the Ugrá, we left the high road and entered narrow country lanes, where green ears of rye bent toward the coach, and the horses managed to bite mouthfuls of grass on either side of the way, as they ran, closely pressed to one another in the narrow, trenchlike road. At last we saw the willows which marked the approach to our village, and suddenly we caught sight of the elegant, pale-yellow bell tower of the Nikólskoye church.

For the quiet life of the landlords of those times Nikólskoye was admirably suited.   There was nothing in it of the luxury which is seen in richer estates ; but an artistic hand was visible in the planning of the buildings and gardens, and in the general arrangement of things.   Besides the main house, which father had recently built, there were, round a spacious and well-kept yard, several smaller houses, which gave a greater degree of independence to their inhabitants, without destroying the close intercourse of the family life.   An immense 'upper garden' was devoted to fruit-trees, and through it the church was reached. The southern slope of the land, which led to the river, was entirely given up to a pleasure garden, where flower-beds were intermingled with alleys of lime-trees, lilacs, and acacias.   From the balcony of the main house there was a beautiful view of the Siréna, with the ruins of an old earthern fortress where the Russians had offered a stubborn resistance during the Mongol invasion, and farther on, the boundless yellow grain-fields, with copses of woods on the horizon.

In the early years of my childhood we occupied with M. Poulain one of the separate houses entirely by ourselves ; and after his method of education was softened by the intervention of our sister Hélène, we were on the best possible terms with him.   Father was invariably absent from home in the summer, which he spent in military inspections, and our stepmother did not pay much attention to us, especially after her own

child, Pauline, was born.   We were thus always with
M. Poulain, who thoroughly enjoyed the stay in the
country, and let us enjoy it.   The woods ; the walks
along the river ; the climbing over the hills to the old
fortress, which M. Poulain made alive for us as he told
how it was defended by the Russians, and how it was
captured by the Tartars ; the little adventures, in one
of which he became our hero by saving Alexander
from drowning ; an occasional encounter with wolves
—there was no end of new and delightful impressions.
Large parties were also organised in which all the
family took part, sometimes picking mushrooms in the
woods, and afterward having tea in the midst of the
forest, where a man a hundred years old lived alone with
his little grandson, taking care of the bees.   At other
times we went to one of father's villages where a big
pond had been dug, in which golden carp were caught
by the thousand—part of them being taken for the landlord and the remainder being distributed among all the
peasants.   My former nurse, Vasilísa, lived in that village.   Her family was one of the poorest ; besides her
husband, she had only a small boy to help her, and a girl,
my foster-sister, who became later on a preacher and a
' Virgin ' in the Nonconformist sect to which they belonged.   There was no bound to her joy when I came
to see her.   Cream, eggs, apples, and honey were all
that she could offer ; but the way in which she offered
them, in bright wooden plates, after having covered the
table with a fine snow-white linen tablecloth of her
own making (with the Russian Nonconformists absolute
cleanliness is a matter of religion), and the fond words
with which she addressed me, treating me as her own

son, left the warmest feelings in my heart. I must say the same of the nurses of my elder brothers, Nicholas and Alexander, who belonged to prominent families of two other Nonconformist sects in Nikólskoye. Few know what treasuries of goodness can be found in the hearts of Russian peasants, even after centuries of the most cruel oppression, which might well have embittered them.

On stormy days M. Poulain had an abundance of tales to tell us, especially about the campaign in Spain. Over and over again we induced him to tell us how he was wounded in a battle, and every time he came to the point when he felt warm blood streaming into his boot, we jumped to kiss him and gave him all sorts of pet names.

Everything seemed to prepare us for the military career: the predilection of our father (the only toys that I remember his having bought for us were a rifle and a real sentry-box); the war tales of M. Poulain; nay, even the library which we had at our disposal. This library, which had once belonged to General Repnínsky, our mother's grandfather, a learned military man of the eighteenth century, consisted exclusively of books on military warfare, adorned with rich plates and beautifully bound in leather. It was our chief recreation, on wet days, to look over the plates of these books, representing the weapons of warfare since the times of the Hebrews, and giving plans of all the battles that had been fought since Alexander of Macedonia. These heavy books also offered excellent materials for building out of them strong fortresses which would stand for some time the blows of a battering-ram and the projectiles of an Archimedean catapult (which, however, persisted in sending stones into the windows, and was soon prohibited). Yet neither Alexander nor I became military men. The literature of the sixties wiped out the teachings of our childhood.

M. Poulain's opinions about revolutions were those of the Orleanist 'Illustration Française,' of which he received back numbers, and of which we knew all the woodcuts. For a long time I could not imagine a revolution otherwise than in the shape of Death riding on a horse, the red flag in one hand and a scythe in the other, mowing down men right and left. So it was pictured in the 'Illustration.' But I now think that M. Poulain's dislike was limited to the uprising of 1848, for one of his tales about the Revolution of 1789 deeply impressed my mind.

The title of prince was used in our house with and without occasion. M. Poulain must have been shocked by it, for he began once to tell us what he knew of the great Revolution. I cannot now recall what he said, but one thing I remember, namely, that 'Count Mirabeau' and other nobles one day renounced their titles, and that Count Mirabeau, to show his contempt for aristocratic pretensions, opened a shop decorated with a signboard which bore the inscription, 'Mirabeau, tailor.' (I tell the story as I had it from M. Poulain.) For a long time after that I worried myself thinking what trade I should take up, so as to write, 'Kropótkin, such and such a handicraft man.' Later on, my Russian teacher, Nikolái Pávlovich Smirnóff, and the general Republican tone of Russian literature influenced me in the same way; and when I began to write novels—that is, in my twelfth year—I adopted the signature P. Kropotkin, which I never have departed from, notwithstanding the remonstrances of my chiefs when I was in the military service.

VIII

In the autumn of 1852 my brother Alexander was sent to the corps of cadets, and from that time we saw each other only during the holidays and occasionally on Sundays. The corps of cadets was six miles from our house, and although we had a dozen horses, it always happened that when the time came to send the sledge to the corps there was no horse free for that purpose. My eldest brother, Nicholas, came home very seldom. The relative freedom which Alexander found at school, and especially the influence of two of his teachers in literature, developed his intellect rapidly, and later on I shall have ample occasion to speak of the beneficial influence that he exercised upon my own development. It is a great privilege to have had a loving, intelligent elder brother.

In the meantime I remained at home. I had to wait till my turn to enter the corps of· pages should come, and that did not happen until I was nearly fifteen years of age. M. Poulain was dismissed, and a German tutor was engaged instead. He was one of those idealistic men who are not uncommon among Germans,

but I remember him chiefly on account of the enthusiastic way in which he used to recite Schiller's poetry,
accompanying it by a most naïve·kind of acting that
delighted me.   He stayed with us only one winter.

The next winter I was sent to attend the classes at
a Moscow gymnasium ; and finally I remained with
our Russian teacher, Smirnóff.   We soon became
friends, especially after my father took both of us for
a journey to his Ryazán estate.   During this journey
we indulged in all sorts of fun, and we used to invent
humorous stories in connection with the men and the
things that we saw ; while the impression produced
upon me by the hilly tracts we crossed added some new
and fine touches to my growing love of nature.   Under
the impulse given me by Smirnóff, my literary tastes
also began to grow, and during the years from 1854 to
1857 I had full opportunity to develop them.   My
teacher, who had by this time finished his studies at
the university, obtained a small clerkship in a law
court, and spent his mornings there.   I was thus left
to myself till dinner-time, and after having prepared my
lessons and taken a walk, I had plenty of leisure for
reading and writing.   In the autumn, when my teacher
returned to his office at Moscow, while we remained in
the country, I was left again to myself, and though in
continual intercourse with the family, and spending
part of the day in playing with my little sister Pauline,
I could in fact dispose of my time as I liked.

Serfdom was then in the last years of its existence.
It is recent history—it seems to be only of yesterday ;
and yet, even in Russia, few realize what serfdom was

in reality. There is a dim conception that the conditions which it created were very bad; but how these conditions affected human beings bodily and mentally is only vaguely understood. It is amazing, indeed, to see how quickly an institution and its social consequences are forgotten when the institution has ceased to exist, and with what rapidity men and things change after that. I will try to recall the conditions of serfdom by telling, not what I heard, but what I saw.

Uliána, the housekeeper, stands in the passage leading to father's room, and crosses herself; she dares neither to advance nor to retreat. At last, after having recited a prayer, she enters the room, and reports, in a hardly audible voice, that the store of tea is nearly at an end, that there are only twenty pounds of sugar left, and that the other provisions will soon be exhausted.

'Thieves, robbers!' shouts my father, 'And you, you are in league with them!' His voice thunders throughout the house. Our stepmother leaves Uliána to face the storm. But father cries, 'Frol, call the princess! Where is she?' And when she enters, he receives her with the same reproaches.

'You also are in league with this progeny of Ham; you are standing up for them;' and so on, for half an hour or more.

Then he commences to verify the accounts. At the same time, he thinks about the hay. Frol is sent to weigh what is left of that, and our stepmother is sent to be present during the weighing, while father calculates how much of it ought to be in the barn. A considerable quantity of hay appears to be missing, and

Uliána cannot account for several pounds of such and such provisions. Father's voice becomes more and more menacing ; Uliána is trembling ; but it is the coachman who now enters the room, and is stormed at by his master. Father springs at him, strikes him, but he keeps repeating, ' Your highness must have made a mistake.'

Father repeats his calculations, and this time it appears that there is more hay in the barn than there ought to be. The shouting continues ; he now reproaches the coachman with not having given the horses their daily rations in full ; but the coachman calls on all the saints to witness that he gave the animals their due, and Frol invokes the Virgin to confirm the coachman's appeal.

But father will not be appeased. He calls in Makár, the piano-tuner and sub-butler, and reminds him of all his recent sins. He was drunk last week, and must have been drunk yesterday, for he broke half a dozen plates. In fact, the breaking of these plates was the real cause of all the disturbance : our step-mother had reported the fact to father in the morning, and that was why Uliána was received with more scolding than was usually the case, why the verification of the hay was undertaken, and why father now continues to shout that ' this progeny of Ham ' deserve all the punishments on earth.

Of a sudden there is a lull in the storm. My father takes his seat at the table and writes a note. ' Take Makár with this note to the police station, and let a hundred lashes with the birch rod be given to him.'

Terror and absolute muteness reign in the house.

The clock strikes four, and we all go down to dinner; but no one has any appetite, and the soup remains in the plates untouched. We are ten at table, and behind each of us a violinist or a trombone-player stands, with a clean plate in his left hand; but Makár is not among them.

'Where is Makár?' our stepmother asks. 'Call him in.'

Makár does not appear, and the order is repeated. He enters at last, pale, with a distorted face, ashamed, his eyes cast down. Father looks into his plate, while our stepmother, seeing that no one has touched the soup, tries to encourage us.

'Don't you find, children,' she says, 'that the soup is delicious?'

Tears suffocate me, and immediately after dinner is over I run out, catch Makár in a dark passage and try to kiss his hand; but he tears it away, and says, either as a reproach or as a question, 'Let me alone; you, too, when you are grown up, will you not be just the same?'

'No, no, never!'

Yet father was not among the worst of landowners. On the contrary, the servants and the peasants considered him one of the best. What we saw in our house was going on everywhere, often in much more cruel forms. The flogging of the serfs was a regular part of the duties of the police and of the fire brigade.

A landowner once made the remark to another, 'Why is it, general, that the number of the souls on your estate increases so slowly? You probably do not look after their marriages.'

A few days later the general ordered that a list of all the inhabitants of his village should be brought him. He picked out from it the names of the boys who had attained the age of eighteen, and of the girls just past sixteen—these are the legal ages for marriage in Russia. Then he wrote, 'John to marry Anna, Paul to marry Paráshka,' and so on with five couples. The five weddings, he added, must take place in ten days, the next Sunday but one.

A general cry of despair rose from the village. Women, young and old, wept in every house. Anna had hoped to marry Gregory ; Paul's parents had already had a talk with the Fedótoffs about their girl, who would soon be of age. Moreover, it was the season for ploughing, not for weddings ; and what wedding can be prepared in ten days ? Dozens of peasants came to see the landowner ; peasant women stood in groups at the back entrance of the mansion, with pieces of fine linen for the landowner's spouse, to secure her intervention. All in vain. The master had said that the weddings should take place at such a date, and so it must be.

At the appointed time, the nuptial processions, in this case more like burial processions, went to the church. The women cried with loud voices, as they are wont to cry during burials. One of the house valets was sent to the church, to report to the master as soon as the wedding ceremonies were over ; but soon he came running back, cap in hand, pale and distressed.

'Paráshka,' he said, 'makes a stand ; she refuses to be married to Paul. Father' (that is, the priest) asked her, " Do you agree ? " but she replied in a loud voice, " No, I don't." '

The landowner grew furious. 'Go and tell that long-maned drunkard ' (meaning the priest ; the Russian clergy wear their hair long) 'that if Paráshka is not married at once, I will report him as a drunkard to the archbishop. How dares he, clerical dirt, disobey me ? Tell him he shall be sent to rot in a monastery, and I shall exile Paráshka's family to the steppes.'

The valet transmitted the message. Paráshka's relatives and the priest surrounded the girl ; her mother, weeping, fell on her knees before her, entreating her not to ruin the whole family. The girl continued to say 'I won't,' but in a weaker and weaker voice, then in a whisper, until at last she stood silent. The nuptial crown was put on her head ; she made no resistance, and the valet ran full speed to the mansion to announce, 'They are married.'

Half an hour later, the small bells of the nuptial processions resounded at the gate of the mansion. The five couples alighted from the cars, crossed the yard and entered the hall. The landlord received them, offering them glasses of wine, while the parents, standing behind the crying daughters, ordered them to bow to the earth before their lord.

Marriages by order were so common that amongst our servants, each time a young couple foresaw that they might be ordered to marry, although they had no mutual inclination for each other, they took the precaution of standing together as godfather and god-mother at the christening of a child in one of the peasant families. This rendered marriage impossible, according to Russian Church law. The stratagem was usually successful, but once it ended in a tragedy. Andréi, the tailor, fell in love with a girl belonging to one of our neighbours. He hoped that my father would permit him to go free, as a tailor, in exchange for a certain yearly payment, and that by working hard at his trade he could manage to lay aside some money and to buy freedom for the girl. Otherwise, in marrying one of my father's serfs she would have become the serf of her husband's master. However, as Andréi and one of the maids of our household foresaw that they might be ordered to marry, they agreed to unite as god-parents in the christening of a child. What they had feared happened : one day they were called to the master, and the dreaded order was given.

' We are always obedient to your will,' they replied, ' but a few weeks ago we acted as godfather and god-mother at a christening.' Andréi also explained his wishes and intentions. The result was that he was sent to the recruiting board to become a soldier.

Under Nicholas I. there was no obligatory military service for all, such as now exists. Nobles and merchants were exempt, and when a new levy of recruits was ordered, the landowners had to supply a certain number of men from their serfs. As a rule, the peasants, within their village communities, kept a roll amongst themselves ; but the house servants were entirely at the mercy of their lord, and if he was dissatisfied with one of them, he sent him to the recruiting board and took a recruit acquittance, which had a considerable money value, as it could be sold to anyone whose turn it was to become a soldier.

Military service in those times was terrible. A man was required to serve twenty-five years under the colours, and the life of a soldier was hard in the extreme. To become a soldier meant to be torn away for ever from one's native village and surroundings, and to be at the mercy of officers like Timoféeff, whom I have already mentioned. Blows from the officers, flogging with birch rods and with sticks, for the slightest fault, were normal affairs. The cruelty that was displayed surpasses all imagination. Even in the corps of cadets, where only noblemen's sons were educated, a thousand blows with birch rods were sometimes administered, in the presence of all the corps, for a cigarette—the doctor standing by the tortured boy, and ordering the punishment to end only when he ascertained that the pulse was about to stop beating. The bleeding victim was carried away unconscious to the hospital. The Grand Duke Mikhael, commander of the military schools, would quickly have removed the director of a corps in which one or two such cases did not occur every year. 'No discipline,' he would have said.

With common soldiers it was far worse. When one of them appeared before a court-martial, the sentence was that a thousand men should be placed in two ranks facing each other, every soldier armed with a stick of the thickness of the little finger (these sticks were known under their German name of *Spitzruthen*), and that the condemned man should be dragged three, four, five, and seven times between these two rows, each soldier adminstering a blow. Sergeants followed to see that full force was used. After one or two thousand blows had been given, the victim, spitting blood, was taken to the hospital and attended to, in order that the punishment might be finished as soon as he had more or less recovered from the effects of the first part of it. If he died under the torture, the execution of the sentence was completed upon the corpse. Nicholas I. and his brother Mikhael were pitiless; no remittance of the punishment was ever possible. 'I will send you through the ranks; you shall be skinned under the sticks,' were threats which made part of the current language.

A gloomy terror used to spread through our house when it became known that one of the servants was to be sent to the recruiting board. The man was chained and placed under guard in the office to prevent suicide. A peasant cart was brought to the office door, and the doomed man was taken out between two watchmen. All the servants surrounded him. He made a deep bow asking everyone to pardon him his willing or un-willing offences. If his father and mother lived in our village, they came to see him off. He bowed to the ground before them, and his mother and his other female relatives began loudly to sing out their lamen-tations—a sort of half-song and half-recitative: 'To whom do you abandon us? Who will take care of you in the strange lands? Who will protect me from cruel men?'—exactly in the same way in which they sang their lamentations at a burial, and with the same words.

Thus Andréi had now to face for twenty-five years the terrible fate of a soldier: all his schemes of happiness had come to a violent end.

The fate of one of the maids, Pauline, or Pólya, as

she used to be called, was even more tragical. She had been apprenticed to make fine embroidery, and was an artist at the work. At Nikólskoye her embroidery frame stood in sister Hélène's room, and she often took part in the conversations that went on between our sister and a sister of our stepmother who stayed with Hélène. Altogether, by her behaviour and talk Pólya was more like an educated young person than a housemaid.

A misfortune befell her: she realized that she would soon be a mother. She told all to our stepmother, who burst into reproaches: 'I will not have that creature in my house any longer! I will not permit such a shame in my house! oh, the shameless creature!' and so on. The tears of Hélène made no difference. Pólya had her hair cut short, and was exiled to the dairy; but as she was just embroidering an extraordinary skirt, she had to finish it at the dairy, in a dirty cottage, at a microscopical window. She finished it, and made many more fine embroideries, all in the hope of obtaining her pardon. But pardon did not come.

The father of her child, a servant of one of our neighbours, implored permission to marry her; but as he had no money to offer, his request was refused. Pólya's 'too gentlewoman-like manners' were taken as an offence, and a most bitter fate was kept in reserve for her. There was in our household a man employed as a postilion, on account of his small size; he went under the name of 'bandy-legged Fílka.' In his boyhood a horse had kicked him terribly, and he did not grow. His legs were crooked, his feet were turned inward, his nose was broken and turned to one side, his jaw was deformed. To this monster it was decided to marry Pólya—and she was married by force. The couple were sent to become peasants at my father's estate in Ryazán.

Human feelings were not recognized, not even suspected, in serfs, and when Turguéneff published his little story 'Mumú,' and Grigoróvich began to issue his thrilling novels, in which he made his readers weep over the misfortunes of the serfs, it was to a great number of persons a startling revelation. 'They love just as we do; is it possible?' exclaimed the sentimental ladies who could not read a French novel without shedding tears over the troubles of the noble heroes and heroines.

The education which the owners occasionally gave to some of their serfs was only another source of misfortune for the latter. My father once picked out in a peasant house a clever boy, and sent him to be educated as a doctor's assistant. The boy was diligent, and after a few years' apprenticeship made a decided success. When he returned home, my father bought all that was required for a well-equipped dispensary, which was arranged very nicely in one of the side houses of Nikólskoye. In summer time Sásha the Doctor—that was the familiar name under which this young man went in the household—was busy gathering and preparing all sorts of medical herbs, and in a short time he became most popular in the region round Nikólskoye. The sick people among the peasants came from the neighbouring villages, and my father was proud of the success of his dispensary. But this condition of things

did not last. One winter, my father came to
Nikólskoye, stayed there for a few days, and left.
That night Sásha the Doctor shot himself—by accident, it was reported; but there was a love story at
the bottom of it. He was in love with a girl whom
he could not marry, as she belonged to another
landowner.

The case of another young man, Gherásim
Kruglóff, whom my father educated at the Moscow
Agricultural Institute, was almost equally sad. He
passed his examinations most brilliantly, getting a gold
medal, and the director of the Institute made all
possible endeavours to induce my father to give him
freedom and to let him go to the university—serfs
not being allowed to enter there. 'He is sure to
become a remarkable man,' the director said, 'perhaps
one of the glories of Russia, and it will be an honour
for you to have recognized his capacities and to
have given such a man to Russian science.'

' I need him for my own estate,' my father replied
to the many applications made on the young man's
behalf. In reality, with the primitive methods of agriculture which were then in use, and from which my
father would never have departed, Gherásim Kruglóff
was absolutely useless. He made a survey of the estate,
but when that was done he was ordered to sit in the
servants' room and to stand with a plate at dinner-time.
Of course Gherásim resented it very much; his dreams
carried him to the university, to scientific work. His
looks betrayed his discontent, and our stepmother
seemed to find an especial pleasure in offending him at
every opportunity. One day in the autumn, a rush of

wind having opened the entrance gate, she called out to him, ' Garáska, go and shut the gate.'

That was the last drop. He answered, ' You have a porter for that,' and went his way.

My stepmother ran into father's room, crying, ' Your servants insult me in your house ! '

Immediately Gherásim was put under arrest, and chained, to be sent away as a soldier. The parting of his old father and mother with him was one of the most heartrending scenes I ever saw.

This time, however, fate took its revenge. Nicholas I. died, and military service became more tolerable. Gherásim's great ability was soon remarked, and in a few years he was one of the chief clerks, and the real working force in one of the departments of the Ministry of War. Meanwhile, my father, who was absolutely honest, and, at a time when almost every one was receiving bribes and making fortunes, had never let himself be bribed, departed once from the strict rules of the service in order to oblige the commander of the corps to which he belonged, and consented to allow an irregularity of some kind. It nearly cost him his promotion to the rank of general; the only object of his thirty-five years' service in the army seemed on the point of being lost. My stepmother went to St. Petersburg to remove the difficulty, and one day, after many applications, she was told that the only way to obtain what she wanted was to address herself to a particular clerk in a certain department of the ministry. Although he was a mere clerk, he was the real head of his superiors, and could do everything. This man's name was Gherásim Ivánovich Kruglóff.

' Imagine, our Garáska ! ' she said to me afterward.
' I always knew that he had great capacity. I went to
see him, and spoke to him about this affair, and he said,
" I have nothing against the old prince, and I will do
all I can for him." '

Gherásim kept his word : he made a favourable
report, and my father got his promotion. At last he
could put on the long-coveted red trousers and the
red-lined overcoat, and could wear the plumage on his
helmet.

These were things which I myself saw in my childhood. If, however, I were to relate what I heard of
in those years it would be a much more gruesome
narrative : stories of men and women torn from their
families and their villages, and sold, or lost in gambling,
or exchanged for a couple of hunting dogs, and then
transported to some remote part of Russia for the sake
of creating a new estate ; of children taken from their
parents and sold to cruel or dissolute masters ; of
flogging ' in the stables,' which occurred every day
with unheard-of cruelty ; of a girl who found her only
salvation in drowning herself ; of an old man who
had grown grey-haired in his master's service, and at
last hanged himself under his master's window ; and of
revolts of serfs, which were suppressed by Nicholas I.'s
generals by flogging to death each tenth or fifth man
taken out of the ranks, and by laying waste the village,
whose inhabitants, after a military execution, went
begging for bread in the neighbouring provinces, as
if they had been the victims of a conflagration. As to
the poverty which I saw during our journeys in certain
villages, especially in those which belonged to the im-

perial family, no words would be adequate to describe the misery to readers who have not seen it.

To become free was the constant dream of the serfs—a dream not easily realized, for a heavy sum of money was required to induce a landowner to part with a serf. 'Do you know,' my father said to me once, ' that your mother appeared to me after her death ? You young people do not believe in these things, but it was so. I sat one night very late in this chair, at my writing-table, and slumbered, when I saw her enter from behind, all in white, quite pale, and with her eyes gleaming. When she was dying she begged me to promise that I would give liberty to her maid, Másha, and I did promise ; but then what with one thing and another, nearly a whole year passed without my having fulfilled my intention. Then she appeared, and said to me in a low voice, " Alexis, you promised me to give liberty to Másha : have you forgotten it ? " - I was quite terrified : I jumped out of my chair, but she had vanished. I called the servants, but no one had seen anything. Next morning I went to her grave and had a litany sung, and immediately gave liberty to Másha.'

When my father died, Másha came to his burial, and I spoke to her. She was married, and quite happy in her family life. My brother Alexander, in his jocose way, told her what my father had said, and we asked her what she knew of it.

' These things,' she replied, ' happened a long time ago, so I may tell you the truth. I saw that your father had quite forgotten his promise, so I dressed up in white and spoke like your mother. I recalled the promise he had made to her—you won't bear a grudge against me, will you?'

'Of course not!'

Ten or twelve years after the scenes described in the early part of this chapter, I sat one night in my father's room, and we talked of things past. Serfdom had been abolished, and my father complained of the new conditions, though not very severely; he had accepted them without much grumbling.

'You must agree, father,' I said, 'that you often punished your servants cruelly, and without any reason.'

'With the people,' he replied, 'it was impossible to do otherwise;' and, leaning back in his easy-chair, he remained plunged in thought. 'But what I did was nothing worth speaking of,' he said after a long pause. 'Take that same Sábleff: he looks so soft, and talks in such a meek voice; but he was really terrible with his serfs. How many times they plotted to kill him! I, at least, never took advantage of my maids, whereas that old devil Tónkoff went on in such a way that the peasant women were going to inflict a terrible punishment upon him. . . . Good-bye; *bonne nuit*!'

IX

I WELL remember the Crimean war. At Moscow it affected people but little. Of course, in every house lint and bandages for the wounded were made at evening parties ; not much of it, however, reached the Russian armies, immense quantities being stolen and sold to the armies of the enemy. My sister Hélène and other young ladies sang patriotic songs, but the general tone of life in society was hardly influenced by the great struggle that was going on. In the country, on the contrary, the war caused much gloominess. The levies of recruits followed one another rapidly, and we continually heard the peasant women singing their funereal songs. The Russian people look upon war as a calamity which is being sent upon them by Providence, and they accepted this war with a solemnity that contrasted strangely with the levity I saw elsewhere under similar circumstances. Young though I was, I realized that feeling of solemn resignation which pervaded our villages.

My brother Nicholas was smitten like many others by the war fever, and before he had ended his course at the corps he joined the army in the Caucasus. I never saw him again.

In the autumn of 1854 our family was increased by the arrival of two sisters of our stepmother. They had had their own house and some vineyards at Sebastopol, but now they were homeless, and came to stay with us. When the allies landed in the Crimea, the inhabitants of Sebastopol were told that they need not be afraid, and had only to stay where they were; but after the defeat at the Alma, they were ordered to leave with all haste, as the city would be invested within a few days. There were few conveyances, and there was no way of moving along the roads in face of the troops which were marching southward. To hire a cart was almost impossible, and the ladies, having abandoned all they had on the road, had a very hard time of it before they reached Moscow.

I soon made friends with the younger of the two sisters, a lady of about thirty, who used to smoke one cigarette after another, and to tell me of all the horrors of their journey. She spoke with tears in her eyes of the beautiful battle-ships which had to be sunk at the entrance of the harbour of Sebastopol, and she could not understand how the Russians would be able to defend Sebastopol from the land; there was no wall even worth speaking of.

I was in my thirteenth year when Nicholas I. died. It was 'late in the afternoon of February 18 (March 2), that the policemen distributed in all the houses of Moscow a bulletin announcing the illness of the Tsar, and inviting the inhabitants to pray in the churches for his recovery. At that time he was already dead, and the authorities knew it, as there was telegraphic communication between Moscow and St. Petersburg; but not a word having been previously uttered about his illness, they thought that the people must be gradually prepared for the announcement of his death. We all went to church and prayed most piously.

'Next day, Saturday, the same thing was done, and even on Sunday morning bulletins about the Tsar's health were distributed. The news of the death of Nicholas reached us only about midday, through some servants who had been to the market. A real terror reigned in our house and in the houses of our relatives, as the information spread. It was said that the people in the market behaved in a strange way, showing no regret, but indulging in dangerous talk. Full-grown people spoke in whispers, and our stepmother kept repeating, 'Don't talk before the men;' while the servants whispered among themselves, probably about the coming 'freedom.' The nobles expected at every moment a revolt of the serfs—a new uprising of Pugachóff.

At St. Petersburg, in the meantime, men of the educated classes, as they communicated to one another the news, embraced in the streets. Everyone felt that the end of the war and the end of the terrible conditions which prevailed under the 'iron despot' were near at hand. Poisoning was talked about, the more so as the Tsar's body decomposed very rapidly, but the true reason only gradually leaked out: a too strong dose of an invigorating medicine that Nicholas had taken.

In the country, during the summer of 1855, the heroic struggle which was going on in Sebastopol for every yard of ground and every bit of its dismantled bastions was followed with a solemn interest. A messenger was sent regularly twice a week from our house to the district town to get the papers; and on his return, even before he had dismounted, the papers were taken from his hands and opened. Hélène or I read them aloud to the family, and the news was at once transmitted to the servants' room, and thence to the kitchen, the office, the priest's house, and the houses of the peasants. The reports which came of the last days of Sebastopol, of the awful bombardment, and finally of the evacuation of the town by our troops were received with tears. In every country house round about, the loss of Sebastopol was mourned over with as much grief as the loss of a near relative would have been, although everyone understood that now the terrible war would soon come to an end.

X

IT was in August 1857, when I was nearly fifteen, that my turn came to enter the corps of pages and I was taken to St. Petersburg. When I left home I was still a child; but human character is usually settled in a definite way at an earlier age than is generally supposed, and it is evident to me that under my childish appearance I was then very much what I was to be later on. My tastes, my inclinations, were already determined.

The first impulse to my intellectual development was given, as I have said, by my Russian teacher. It is an excellent habit in Russian families—a habit now, unhappily, on the decline—to have in the house a student who aids the boys and the girls with their lessons, even

when they are at a gymnasium. For a better assimila-
tion of what they learn at school, and for a widening of
their conceptions about what they learn, his aid is
invaluable. Moreover, he introduces an intellectual
element into the family and becomes an elder brother
to the young people—often something better than an
elder brother, because the student has a certain responsibility for the progress of his pupils ; and as the
methods of teaching change rapidly, from one generation to another, he can assist his pupils much better
than the best educated parents could.

Nikolái Pávlovich Smirnóff had literary tastes. At
that time, under the wild censorship of Nicholas I.,
many quite inoffensive works by our best writers could
not be published ; others were so mutilated as to de-
prive many passages in them of any meaning. In the
genial comedy by Griboyédoff, ' Misfortune from
Intelligence,' which ranks with the best comedies of
Molière, Colonel Skalozúb had to be named ' Mr.
Skalozúb,' to the detriment of the sense and even of
the verses ; for the representation of a colonel in a comical light would have been considered an insult to the
army. Of so innocent a book as Gógol's ' Dead Souls '
the second part was not allowed to appear, nor the
first part to be reprinted, although it had long been out
of print. Numerous verses of Púshkin, Lérmontoff,
A. K. Tolstóy, Ryléeff, and other poets were not permitted to see the light ; to say nothing of such verses
as had any political meaning or contained a criticism
of the prevailing conditions. All these circulated in
manuscript, and my teacher used to copy whole books of
Gógol and Púshkin for himself and his friends, a task

in which I occasionally helped him. As a true child of Moscow he was also imbued with the deepest veneration for those of our writers who lived in Moscow—some of them in the Old Equerries' Quarter. He pointed out to me with respect the house of the Countess Saliás (Eugénie Tour), who was our near neighbour, while the house of the noted exile Alexander Hérzen always was associated with a certain mysterious feeling of respect and awe. The house where Gógol lived was for us an object of deep respect, and though I was not nine when he died (in 1851), and had read none of his works, I remember well the sadness his death produced at Moscow. Turguéneff well expressed that feeling in a note, for which Nicholas I. ordered him to be put under arrest and sent into exile to his estate.

Púshkin's great poem, 'Evghéniy Onyéghin,' made but little impression upon me, and I still admire the marvellous simplicity and beauty of his style in that poem more than its contents. But Gógol's works, which I read when I was eleven or twelve, had a powerful effect on my mind, and my first literary essays were in imitation of his humorous manner. An historical novel by Zagóskin, 'Yúriy Miloslávskiy,' about the times of the great uprising of 1612, Púshkin's 'The Captain's Daughter,' dealing with the Pugachóff uprising, and Dumas' 'Queen Marguerite' awakened in me a lasting interest in history. As to other French novels, I have only begun to read them since Daudet and Zola came to the front. Nekrásoff's poetry was my favourite from early years : I knew many of his verses by heart.

Nikolái Pávlovich Smirnóff early began to make me

write, and with his aid I wrote a long 'History of a Six-pence,' for which we invented all sorts of characters, into whose possession the sixpence fell.

My brother Alexander had at that time a much more poetical turn of mind. He wrote most romantic stories, and began early to make verses, which he did with wonderful facility and in a most musical and easy style. If his mind had not subsequently been taken up by natural history and philosophical studies, he undoubtedly would have become a poet of mark. In those years his favourite resort for finding poetical inspiration was the gently sloping roof underneath our window. This aroused in me a constant desire to tease him. 'There is the poet sitting under the chimney-pot, trying to write his verses,' I used to say ; and the teasing ended in a fierce scrimmage, which brought our sister Hélène to a state of despair. But Alexander was so devoid of revengefulness that peace was soon concluded, and we loved each other immensely. Among boys, scrimmage and love seem to go hand in hand.

I had even then taken to journalism. In my twelfth year I began to edit a daily journal. Paper was not to be had at will in our house, and my journal was of a Liliputian size. As the Crimean war had not yet broken out, and the only newspaper which my father used to receive was the Gazette of the Moscow Police, I had not a great choice of models. As a result my own Gazette consisted merely of short paragraphs announcing the news of the day : as, ' Went out to the woods. N. P. Smirnóff shot two thrushes,' and the like.

This soon ceased to satisfy me, and in 1855 I

started a monthly review which contained Alexander's verses, my novelettes, and some sort of 'varieties.' The material existence of this review was fully guaranteed, for it had plenty of subscribers; that is, the editor himself and Smirnóff, who regularly paid his subscription, of so many sheets of paper, even after he had left our house. In return, I accurately wrote out for my faithful subscriber a second copy.

When Smirnóff left us, and a student of medicine, N. M. Pávloff, took his place, the latter helped me in my editorial duties. He obtained for the review a poem by one of his friends, and—still more important—the introductory lecture on physical geography by one of the Moscow professors. Of course this had not been printed before : a reproduction would never have found its way into so serious a publication.

Alexander, I need not say, took a lively interest in the review, and its renown soon reached the corps of cadets. Some young writers on the way to fame undertook the publication of a rival. The matter was serious : in poems and novels we could hold our own ; but they had a 'critic,' and a 'critic' who writes, in connection with the characters of some new novel, all sorts of things about the conditions of life, and touches upon a thousand questions which could not be touched upon anywhere else, makes the soul of a Russian review. They had a critic, and we had none ! Happily enough, the article he wrote for the first number was shown to my brother. It was rather pretentious and weak, and Alexander at once wrote an anti-criticism, ridiculing and demolishing the critic in a violent manner. There was great consternation in the rival camp when they learned that this anti-criticism would appear in our next issue ; they gave up publishing their review and their best writers joined our staff. We triumphantly announced the future ' exclusive collaboration ' of so many distinguished writers.

In August 1857 the review had to be suspended, after nearly two years' existence. New surroundings and a quite new life were before me. I went away from home with regret, the more so because the whole distance between Moscow and St. Petersburg would be between me and Alexander, and I already considered it a misfortune that I had to enter a military school.

INTRODUCTION

PART SECOND

THE CORPS OF PAGES

I

THE long-cherished ambition of my father was thus realized. There was a vacancy in the corps of pages which I could fill before I had got beyond the age to which admission was limited, and I was taken to St. Petersburg and entered the school. Only a hundred and fifty boys—mostly children of the nobility belonging to the court—received education in this privileged corps, which combined the character of a military school endowed with special rights and of a court institution attached to the imperial household. After a stay of four or five years in the corps of pages, those who had passed the final examinations were received as officers in any regiment of the Guard or of the army they chose, irrespective of the number of vacancies in that regiment; and each year the first sixteen pupils of the highest form were nominated *pages de chambre* : that is, they were personally attached to the several members of the imperial family—the emperor, the empress, the grand duchesses, and the grand dukes. That was considered, of course, a great honour ; and, moreover, the young men upon whom this honour was bestowed became known at the court, and had afterward every chance of being nominated aides-de-camp of the emperor or of one of the grand dukes, and consequently had every facility for making a brilliant career in the service of the State. Fathers and mothers took due care, therefore, that their boys should not miss entering the corps of pages, even though entrance had to be secured at the expense of other candidates who never saw a vacancy opening for them. Now that I was · in the select corps my father could give free play to his ambitious dreams.

The corps was divided into five forms, of which the highest was the first, and the lowest the fifth, and the intention was that I should enter the fourth form. However, as it appeared at the examinations that I was not sufficiently familiar with decimal fractions, and as the fourth form contained that year over forty pupils, while only twenty had been mustered for the fifth form, I was enrolled in the latter.

I felt extremely vexed at this decision. It was with reluctance that I entered a military school, and now I should have to stay in it five years instead of four. What should I do in the fifth form, when I knew already all that would be taught in it? With tears in my eyes I spoke of it to the inspector (the head of the educational department), but he answered me with a joke. 'You know,' he told me, 'what Cæsar said— better to be the first in a village than the second in Rome.' To which I warmly replied that I should prefer to be the very last if only I could leave the military school as soon as possible. 'Perhaps, after some time, you will like the school,' he remarked, and from that day he became friendly to me.

To the teacher of arithmetic, who also tried to console me, I gave my word of honour that I would never cast a glance into his textbook; 'and never-

theless you will have to give me the highest marks.'
I kept my word; but thinking now of this scene,
I fancy that the pupil was not of a very docile dis-
position.

And yet, as I look back upon that remote past, I
cannot but feel grateful for having been put in the
lower form. Having only to repeat during the first
year what I already knew, I got into the habit of
learning my lessons by merely listening to what the
teachers said in the class-room; and, the lessons over,
I had plenty of time to read and to write to my heart's
content. I never prepared for the examinations, and
used to spend the time which was allowed for that in
reading aloud to a few friends the dramas of Shake-
speare or of Ostróvskiy. When I reached the higher
'special' forms, I was also better prepared to master
the variety of subjects we had to study. Besides,
I spent more than half of the first winter in the hospital.
Like all children who are not born at St. Petersburg,
I had to pay a heavy tribute to 'the capital on the
swamps of Finland,' in the shape of several attacks of
local cholera, and finally one of typhoid fever.

When I entered the corps of pages, its inner life was
undergoing a profound change. All Russia awakened
at that time from the heavy slumber and the terrible
nightmare of Nicholas I.'s reign. Our school also felt
the effects of that revival. I do not know, in fact,
what would have become of me, had I entered the corps
of pages one or two years sooner. Either my will
would have been totally broken, or I should have been
excluded from the school with no one knows what

consequences.   Happily, the transition period was already in full sway in the year 1857.

The director of the corps was an excellent old man, General Zheltúkhin.   But he was the nominal head only.   The real master of the school was ' the Colonel,' —Colonel Girardot, a Frenchman in the Russian service.   People said he was a Jesuit, and so he was, I believe.   His ways, at any rate, were thoroughly imbued with the teachings of Loyola, and his educational methods were those of the French Jesuit colleges.

Imagine a short, extremely thin man, with dark, piercing, and furtive eyes, wearing short clipped moustaches, which gave him the expression of a cat ; very quiet and firm ; not remarkably intelligent, but exceedingly cunning ; a despot at the bottom of his heart, who was capable of hating—intensely hating— the boy who would not fall under his fascination, and of expressing that hatred, not by silly persecutions, but unceasingly by his general behaviour—by an occcasionally dropped word, a gesture, a smile, an interjection. His walk was more like gliding along, and the exploring glances he used to cast round without turning his head completed the illusion.   A stamp of cold dryness was impressed on his lips, even when he tried to look well disposed, and that expression became still more harsh when his mouth was contorted by a smile of discontent or of contempt.   With all this there was nothing of a commander in him ; you would rather think, at first sight, of a benevolent father who talks to his children as if they were full-grown people.   And yet, you soon felt that everyone and everything had to bend before his will.   Woe to the boy who would not feel happy or unhappy according to the degree of good disposition shown toward him by the Colonel.

The words ' the Colonel' were continually on all lips. Other officers went by their nicknames, but no one dared to give a nickname to Girardot. A sort of mystery hung about him, as if he were omniscient and everywhere present. True, he spent all the day and part of the night in the school. Even when we were in the classes he prowled about, visiting our drawers, which he opened with his own keys. As to the night, he gave a good portion of it to the task of inscribing in small books—of which he had quite a library—in separate columns, by special signs and in inks of different colours, all the faults and virtues of each boy.

Play, jokes, and conversations stopped when we saw him slowly moving along through our spacious rooms, hand in hand with one of his favourites, balancing his body forward and backward; smiling at one boy, keenly looking into the eyes of another, casting an indifferent glance upon a third, and giving a slight contortion to his lip as he passed a fourth : and from these looks everyone knew that he liked the first boy, that to the second he was indifferent, that he intentionally did not notice the third, and that he disliked the fourth. This dislike was enough to terrify most of his victims—the more so as no reason could be given for it. Impressionable boys had been brought to despair by that mute, unceasingly displayed aversion and those suspicious looks ; in others the result had been a total annihilation of will, as one of the Tolstóys— Theodor, also a pupil of Girardot—has shown in an autobiographic novel, the 'Diseases of the Will.'.

The inner life of the corps was miserable under the rule of the Colonel. In all boarding-schools the newly entered boys are subjected to petty persecutions. The 'greenhorns' are put in this way to a test. What are they worth? Are they not going to turn 'sneaks'? And then the 'old hands' like to show to new-comers the superiority of an established brotherhood. So it is in all schools and in prisons. But under Girardot's rule these persecutions took on a harsher aspect, and they came, not from the comrades of the same form, but from the first form—the pages de chambre, who were non-commissioned officers, and whom Girardot had placed in a quite exceptional, superior position. His system was to give them carte blanche; to pretend that he did not know even the horrors they were enacting; and to maintain through them a severe discipline. To answer a blow received from a page de chambre would have meant, in the times of Nicholas I., to be sent to a battalion of soldiers' sons, if the fact became public; and to revolt in any way against the mere caprice of a page de chambre meant that the twenty youths of the first form, armed with their heavy oak rulers, would assemble in a room, and, with Girardot's tacit approval, administer a severe beating to the boy who had shown such a spirit of insubordination.

Accordingly, the first form did what they liked; and not farther back than the preceding winter one of their favourite games had been to assemble the 'greenhorns' at night in a room, in their night-shirts, and to make them run round, like horses in a circus, while the pages de chambre, armed with thick india-rubber whips, standing some in the centre and the others on the outside, pitilessly whipped the boys. As a rule the ' circus' ended in an Oriental fashion, in an abominable way. The moral conceptions which prevailed at that time, and the foul talk which went on in the school concerning what occurred at night after a circus, were such that the least said about them the better.

The Colonel knew all this. He had a perfectly organized system of espionage, and nothing escaped his knowledge. But so long as he was not known to know it, all was right. To shut his eyes to what was done by the first form was the foundation of his system of maintaining discipline.

However, a new spirit was awakened in the school, and only a few months before I entered it a revolution had taken place. That year the third form was different from what it had hitherto been. It contained a number of young men who really studied, and read a good deal; some of them became, later, men of mark. My first acquaintance with one of them—let me call him von Schauff—was when he was reading Kant's ' Critique of Pure Reason.' Besides, they had amongst them some of the strongest youths of the school. The tallest member of the corps was in that form, as also a very strong young man, Kóshtoff, a great friend of von Schauff.

This third form did not bear the yoke of the pages de chambre with the same docility as their predecessors ; they were disgusted with what was going on, and in consequence of an incident, which I prefer not to describe, a fight took place between the third and the first form, with the result that the pages de chambre got a severe thrashing from their subordinates. Girardot hushed up the affair, but the authority of the first form was broken down. The india-rubber whips remained, but were never again brought into use. The circuses and the like became things of the past.

That much was won ; but the lowest form, the fifth, composed almost entirely of very young boys who had just entered the school, had still to obey the petty caprices of the pages de chambre. We had a beautiful garden, filled with old trees, but the boys of the fifth form could enjoy it little; they were forced to run a roundabout, while the first form boys sat in it and chattered, or to send back the balls when these gentlemen played nine-pins. A couple of days after I had entered the school, seeing how things stood in the garden, I did not go there, but remained upstairs. I was reading, when a page de chambre, with carroty hair and a face covered with freckles, came upon me, and ordered me to go at once to the garden to run the roundabout.

'I sha'n't; don't you see I am reading,' was my reply.

Anger disfigured his never too pleasant face. He was ready to jump upon me. I took the defensive. He tried to give me blows on the face with his cap. I fenced as best I could. Then he flung his cap on the floor.

'Pick it up.'

'Pick it up yourself.'

Such an act of disobedience was unheard of in the

school. Why he did not beat me unmercifully on the spot I do not know. He was much older and stronger than I was.

Next day and the following days I received similar commands, but obstinately remained upstairs. Then began the most exasperating petty persecutions at every step—enough to drive a boy to desperation. Happily, I was always of a jovial disposition, and answered them with jokes, or took little heed of them.

Moreover, it all soon came to an end. The weather turned rainy, and we spent most of our time indoors. In the garden the first form smoked freely enough, but when we were indoors the smoking club was ' the tower.' It was kept beautifully clean, and a fire was always burning there. The pages de chambre severely punished any of the other boys whom they caught smoking, but they themselves sat continually at the fireside chattering and enjoying cigarettes. Their favourite smoking time was after ten o'clock at night, when all were supposed to have gone to bed; they kept up their·club till half-past eleven, and, to protect themselves from an unexpected interruption by Girardot, they ordered us to be on the watch. The small boys of the fifth form were taken out of their beds in turn, two at a time, and they had to loiter about the staircase till half-past eleven, to give nòtice of the approach of the Colonel.

We decided to put an end to these night watches. Long were the discussions, and the higher forms were consulted as to what was to be done. At last the decision came : ' Refuse, all of you, to keep the watch ; and when they begin to beat you, which they are sure to

do, go, as many of you as you can, in a block, and call in
Girardot. He knows it all, but then he will be bound
to stop it.' The question whether that would not be
' reporting ' was settled in the negative by experts in
matters of honour : the pages de chambre did not
behave towards the others like comrades.

The turn to watch fell that night to a Prince
Shahovskóy, an old hand, and to Selánoff, a new-comer,
an extremely timid boy, who even spoke in a girlish
voice. The old hand was called upon first, but refused
to go, and was left alone. Then two pages de chambre
went to the timid new-comer, who was in bed ; and as
he refused to obey, they began to flog him brutally with
heavy leather braces. Shahovskóy woke up several
comrades who were near at hand, and they all ran to
find Girardot.

I was also in bed when the two came upon me,
ordering me to take the watch. I refused. Thereupon,
seizing two pairs of braces—we always used to put our
clothes in perfect order on a bench by the bedside,
braces uppermost, and the necktie across them—they
began to flog me. Sitting up in bed, I fenced with my
hands, and had already received several heavy blows,
when a command resounded, ' The first form to the
Colonel ! ' The fierce fighters became tame at once,
and hurriedly put my things in order.

' Don't say a word,' they whispered.

' The necktie across, in good order,' I said to them,
while my shoulders and arms burned from the blows.

What Girardot's talk with the first form was we
did not know ; but next day, as we stood in the ranks
before marching downstairs to the dining-room, he

addressed us in a minor key, saying how sad it was
that pages de chambre should have fallen upon a boy
who was right in his refusal. And upon whom? A
new-comer, and so timid a boy as Selánoff was! The
whole school was disgusted at this Jesuitic speech.

It surely was also a blow to Girardot's authority,
and he resented it very much. He regarded our form,
and me especially, with great dislike (the roundabout
affair had been reported to him), and he manifested it
at every opportunity.

During the first winter I was a frequent inmate of
the hospital. After suffering from typhoid fever,
during which the director and the doctor bestowed on
me a really parental care, I had very bad and persis-
tently recurring gastric attacks. Girardot, as he made
his daily rounds of the hospital, seeing me so often
there, began to say to me every morning, half-jokingly,
in French, 'Here is a young man who is as healthy as
the New Bridge, and loiters in the hospital.' Once or
twice I replied jestingly, but at last, seeing malice in
this constant repetition, I lost patience and grew very
angry.

'How dare you say that?' I exclaimed. 'I shall
ask the doctor to forbid your entering this room,' and
so on.

Girardot recoiled two steps; his dark eyes glittered,
his thin lip became still thinner. At last he said, 'I
have offended you, have I? Well, we have in the hall
two artillery guns : shall we have a duel?'

'I don't make jokes, and I tell you that I shall bear
no more of your insinuations,' I continued.

He did not repeat his joke, but regarded me with even more dislike than before.

Happily enough, there was little opportunity for punishing me. I did not smoke; my clothes were always hooked and buttoned, and properly folded at night. I liked all sorts of games, but, plunged as I was in reading and in a correspondence with my brother, I could hardly find time to play a *laptá* match (a sort of cricket) in the garden, and always hurried back to my books. But when I was caught in fault, it was not I that Girardot punished, but the page de chambre who was my superior. Once, for instance, at dinner, I made a physical discovery: I noticed that the sound given out by a tumbler depends on the amount of water it contains, and at once tried to obtain a chord with four glasses. But there stood Girardot behind me, and without saying a word to me he ordered my page de chambre under arrest. It so happened that this young man was an excellent fellow, a third cousin of mine, who refused even to listen to my excuses, saying, 'All right. I know he dislikes you.' His comrades, though, gave me a warning. 'Take care, naughty boy; we are not going to be punished for you,' they said; and if reading had not been my all-absorbing occupation, they probably would have made me pay dearly for my physical experiment.

Everyone spoke of Girardot's dislike for me; but I paid no attention to it, and probably increased it by my indifference. For full eighteen months he refused to give me the epaulettes, which were usually given to newly entered boys after one or two months' stay at the school, when they had learned some of the rudiments

of military drill ; but I felt quite happy without that
military decoration. At last, an officer—the best
teacher of drill in the school, a man simply enamoured
of drill—volunteered to teach me ; and when he saw
me performing all the tricks to his entire satisfaction,
he undertook to introduce me to Girardot. The Colonel
refused again, twice in succession, so that the officer
took it as a personal offence ; and when the director of
the corps once asked him why I had no epaulettes
yet, he bluntly answered, ' The boy is all right ; it is
the Colonel who does not want him ; ' whereupon,
probably after the remark of the director, Girardot
himself asked to examine me again, and gave me the
epaulettes that very day.

But the Colonel's influence was rapidly vanishing.
The whole character of the school was changing. For
twenty years Girardot had realized his ideal, which was
to have the boys nicely combed, curled, and girlish
looking, and to send to the court pages as refined as
courtiers of Louis XIV. Whether they learned or not,
he cared little ; his favourites were those whose clothes-
basket was best filled with all sorts of nail-brushes and
scent-bottles, whose ' private ' uniform (which could be
put on when we went home on Sundays) was of the
best make, and who knew how to make the most elegant
salut oblique. Formerly, when Girardot had held rehearsals of court ceremonies, wrapping up a page in a
striped red cotton cover taken from one of our beds, in
order that he might represent the Empress at a
baisemain, the boys almost religiously approached the
imaginary Empress, seriously performed the ceremony
of kissing the hand, and retired with a most elegant

oblique bow; but now, though they were very elegant
at court, they would perform at the rehearsals such
bearlike bows that all roared with laughter, while
Girardot was simply raging. Formerly, the younger
boys who had been taken to a court levee, and had been
curled for that purpose, used to keep their curls as
long as they would last; now, on returning from
the palace, they hurried to put their heads under the
cold water tap, to get rid of the curls. An effeminate
appearance was laughed at. To be sent to a levee, to
stand there as a decoration, was now considered a
drudgery rather than a favour. And when the small
boys who were occasionally taken to the palace to
play with the little grand dukes remarked that one of
the latter used, in some game, to make a hard whip out
of his handkerchief, and use it freely, one of our boys did
the same, and so whipped the grand duke that he cried.
Girardot was terrified, while the old Sebastopol admiral
who was tutor of the grand duke only praised our boy.

·A new spirit, studious and serious, developed in the
corps, as in all other schools. In former years, the pages,
being sure in one way or another that they would get
the necessary marks for being promoted officers of the
Guard, spent the first years in the school hardly learning
at all, and only began to study more or less in the last
two forms; now the lower forms learned very well.
The moral tone also became quite different from what
it was a few years before. Oriental amusements were
looked upon with disgust, and an attempt or two to
revert to old manners resulted in scandals which
reached the St. Petersburg drawing-rooms. Girardot
was dismissed. He was only allowed to retain his

bachelor apartment in the building of the corps, and we often saw him afterward, wrapped in his long military cloak, pacing along, plunged in reflections—sad, I suppose, because he could not but condemn the new spirit which rapidly developed in the corps of pages.

II

ALL over Russia people were talking of education. As soon as peace had been concluded at Paris, and the severity of censorship had been slightly relaxed, educational matters began to be eagerly discussed. The ignorance of the masses of the people, the obstacles that had hitherto been put in the way of those who wanted to learn, the absence of schools in the country, the obsolete methods of teaching, and the remedies for these evils became favourite themes of discussion in educated circles, in the press, and even in the drawing-rooms of the aristocracy. The first high schools for girls had been opened in 1857, on an excellent plan and with a splendid teaching staff. As by magic a number of men and women came to the front who have not only devoted their lives to education, but have proved to be remarkable practical pedagogists : their writings would occupy a place of honour in every civilized literature, if they were known abroad.

The corps of pages also felt the effect of that revival. Apart from a few exceptions, the general tendency of the three younger forms was to study. The head of the educational department, the inspector, Winkler, who was a well-educated colonel of artillery, a good mathematician, and a man of progressive opinions, hit upon an excellent plan for stimulating that spirit. Instead of the indifferent teachers who formerly used to teach in the lower forms, he endeavoured to secure the best ones. In his opinion, no professor was too good to teach the very beginnings of a subject to the youngest boys. Thus, to teach the elements of algebra in the fourth form he invited a first-rate mathematician and a born teacher, Captain Sukhónin, and the form took at once to mathematics. By the way, it so happened that this captain was a tutor of the heir of the throne (Nikolái Alexándrovich, who died at the age of twenty-two), and the heir-apparent was brought once a week to the corps of pages to be present at the algebra lessons of Captain Sukhónin. The Empress Marie Alexándrovna, who was an educated woman, thought that perhaps the contact with studious boys would stimulate her son to learning. He sat among us, and had to answer questions like all the others. But he managed mostly, while the teacher spoke, to make drawings, very nicely, or to whisper all sorts of droll things to his neighbours. He was good-natured and very gentle in his behaviour, but superficial in learning and still more so in his affections.

For the fifth form the inspector secured two remarkable men. He entered our class-room, one day, quite radiant, and told us that we should have a rare chance. Professor Klasóvsky, a great classical scholar and expert in Russian literature, had consented to teach us Russian grammar, and would take us through all the five forms in succession, shifting with us every year to the next form. Another university professor, Herr Becker, librarian of the imperial (national) library, would do the same in German. Professor Klasóvsky, he added, was in weak health that winter, but the inspector was sure that we would be very quiet in his class. The chance of having such a teacher was too good to be lost.

He had thought aright. We became very proud of having university professors for teachers, and although there came voices from the Kamchátka (in Russia, the back benches of each class bear the name of that remote and uncivilized peninsula) to the effect that ' the sausage-maker '—that is, the German—must be kept by all means in obedience, public opinion in our form was decidedly in favour of the professors.

' The sausage-maker ' won our respect at once. A tall man, with an immense forehead and very kind, intelligent eyes, slightly veiled by his spectacles, came into our class, and told us in quite good Russian that he intended to divide our form into three sections. The first section would be composed of Germans, who already knew the language, and from whom he would require more serious work ; to the second section he would teach grammar, and later on German literature, in accordance with the established programmes ; and the third section, he concluded with a charming smile, would be the Kamchátka. ' From you,' he said, ' I shall only require that at each lesson you copy four lines which I will choose for you from a book. The four lines copied, you can do what you like ; only do not hinder the rest. And I promise you that in five years you

н 2

will learn something of German and German literature. Now, who joins the Germans? You, Stackelberg? You, Lamsdorf? Perhaps some one of the Russians? And who joins the Kamchátka?' Five or six boys, who knew not a word of German, took residence in the peninsula. They most conscientiously copied their four lines—a dozen or a score of lines in the higher forms—and Becker chose the lines so well, and bestowed so much attention upon the boys that by the end of the five years they really knew something of the language and its literature.

I joined the Germans. My brother Alexander insisted so much in his letters upon my acquiring German, which possesses so rich a literature and into which every book of value is translated, that I set myself assiduously to learn it. I translated and studied most thoroughly one page of a rather difficult poetical description of a thunderstorm; I learned by heart, as the professor had advised me, the conjugations, the adverbs, and the prepositions—and began to read. A splendid method it is for learning languages. Becker advised me, moreover, to subscribe to a cheap illustrated weekly, and its illustrations and short stories were a continual inducement to read a few lines or a column. I soon mastered the language.

Toward the end of the winter I asked Herr Becker to lend me a copy of Goethe's 'Faust.' I had read it in a Russian translation; I had also read Turguéneff's beautiful novel, 'Faust'; and I now longed to read the great work in the original. 'You will understand nothing in it; it is too philosophical,' Becker said, with his gentle smile; but he brought me, nevertheless, a little square book, with the pages yellowed by age, containing the immortal drama. He little knew the unfathomable joy that that small square book gave me. I drank in the sense and the music of every line of it, beginning with the very first verses of the ideally beautiful dedication, and soon knew full pages by heart. Faust's monologue in the forest, and especially the lines in which he speaks of his understanding of nature,

> Thou
> Not only cold, amazed acquaintance yield'st,
> But grantest that in her profoundest breast
> I gaze, as in the bosom of a friend,

simply put me in ecstasy, and till now it has retained ts power over me. Every verse gradually became a dear friend. And then, is there a higher æsthetic delight than to read poetry in a language which one does not quite thoroughly understand? The whole is veiled with a sort of slight haze, which admirably suits poetry. Words, the trivial meanings of which, when one knows the language colloquially, sometimes interfere with the poetical image they are intended to convey, retain but their subtle, elevated sense; while the music of the poetry is only the more strongly impressed upon the ear.

Professor Klasóvsky's first lesson was a revelation to us. He was a small man, about fifty years of age, very rapid in his movements, with bright, intelligent eyes, a slightly sarcastic expression, and the high forehead of a poet. When he came in for his first lesson, he said in a low voice that, suffering from a protracted illness, he could not speak loud enough, and asked us, therefore, to sit closer to him.   He placed his chair near the first row of tables, and we clustered round him like a swarm of bees.

He was to teach us Russian grammar ; but, instead of the dull grammar lesson, we heard something quite different from what we expected.   It was grammar : but here came in a comparison of an old Russian folklore expression with a line from Homer or from the Sanskrit Mahabharata, the beauty of which was rendered in Russian words ; there, a verse from Schiller was introduced, and was followed by a sarcastic remark about some modern society prejudice; then solid grammar again, and then some wide poetical or philosophical generalization.

Of course, there was much in it that we did not understand, or of which we missed the deeper sense. But do not the bewitching powers of all studies lie in that they continually open up to us new and unsuspected horizons, not yet understood, which entice us to proceed farther and farther in the penetration of what appears at first sight only in vague outline ?   Some with their hands placed on one another's shoulders, some leaning across the tables of the first row, others standing close behind Klasóvsky, we all hung on his lips. As toward the end of the hour his voice fell, the more breathlessly we listened.   The inspector opened the door of the class-room, to see how we behaved with our new teacher ; but on seeing that motionless swarm he retired on tiptoe.   Even Daúroff, a restless spirit, stared at Klasóvsky as if to say, ' That is the sort of man you are ? '   Even von Kleinau, a hopelessly obtuse Circassian with a German name, sat motionless.   In most of the others something good and elevated simmered at the bottom of their hearts, as if a vision of an unsuspected world was opening before them. Upon me Klasóvsky had an immense influence, which only grew with years. Winkler's prophecy, that, after all, I might like the school, was fulfilled.

In western Europe, and probably in America, this type of teacher seems not to be widely spread; but in Russia there is not a man or woman of mark, in literature or in political life, who does not owe the first impulse toward a higher development to his or her teacher of literature. Every school in the world ought to have such a teacher. Each teacher in a school has his own subject, and there is no link between the different subjects. Only the teacher of literature, guided by the general outlines of the programme, but left free to treat it as he likes, can bind together the separate historical ·and humanitarian sciences, unify them by a broad philosophical and humane conception, and awaken higher ideas and inspirations in the brains and hearts of young people. In Russia, that necessary task falls quite naturally upon the teacher of Russian literature. As he speaks of the development of the language, of the contents of the early epic poetry, of popular songs and music, and, later on, of modern fiction, of the scientific, political, and philosophical literature of his own country, and the divers æsthetical, political, and philosophical currents it has reflected, he is bound to introduce that generalized conception of the development of the human mind which lies beyond the scope of each of the subjects that are taught separately.

The same thing ought to be done for the natural sciences as well.   It is not enough to teach physics and chemistry, astronomy and meteorology, zoology and botany.   The philosophy of all the natural sciences—a general view of nature as a whole, something on the lines of the first volume of Humboldt's ' Cosmos '—must be conveyed to the pupils and the students, whatsoever may be the extension given to the study of the natural sciences in the school.   The philosophy and the poetry of nature, the methods of all the exact sciences, and an inspired conception of the life of nature must make part of education.   Perhaps the teacher of geography might provisionally assume this function ; but then we should require quite a different set of teachers of this subject, and a different set of professors of geography in the universities would be needed.   What is now taught under this name is anything you like, but it is not geography.

Another teacher conquered our rather uproarious form in a quite different manner.   It was the teacher of writing, the last one of the teaching staff.   If the ' heathen '—that is, the German and the French teachers—were regarded with little respect, the teacher of writing, Ebert, who was a German Jew, was a real martyr.   To be insolent with him was a sort of *chic* amongst the pages.   His poverty alone must have been the reason why he kept to his lesson in our corps. The old hands, who had stayed for two or three years in the fifth form without moving higher up, treated him very badly ; but by some means or other he had made an agreement with them : ' One frolic during each lesson, but no more '—an agreement which, I am afraid, was not always honestly kept on our side.

One day, one of the residents of the remote peninsula soaked the blackboard sponge with ink and chalk and flung it at the caligraphy martyr. ' Get it, Ebert ! ' he shouted, with a stupid smile. The sponge touched Ebert's shoulder, the grimy ink spirted into his face and down on to his white shirt.

We were sure that this time Ebert would leave the room and report the fact to the inspector. But he only exclaimed, as he took out his cotton handkerchief and wiped his face, ' Gentlemen, one frolic—no more to-day ! The shirt is spoiled,' he added in a subdued voice, and continued to correct someone's book.

We looked stupefied and ashamed. Why, instead of reporting, he had thought at once of the agreement ! The feelings of the whole class turned in his favour. ' What you have done is stupid,' we reproached our comrade. ' He is a poor man, and you have spoiled his shirt ! Shame ! ' somebody cried.

The culprit went at once to make excuses. ' One must learn, sir,' was all that Ebert said in reply, with sadness in his voice.

All became silent after that, and at the next lesson, as if we had settled it beforehand, most of us wrote in our best possible handwriting, and took our books to Ebert, asking him to correct them. He was radiant, he felt happy that day.

This fact deeply impressed me, and was never wiped out from my memory. To this day I feel grateful to that remarkable man for his lesson.

With our teacher of drawing, who was named Ganz, we never arrived at living on good terms. He continually reported those who played in his class. This, in our opinion, he had no right to do, because he was only a teacher of drawing, but especially because he was not an honest man. In the class he paid little attention to most of us, and spent his time in improving the drawings of those who took private lessons from him, or paid him in order to show at the examinations a good drawing and to get a good mark for it. Against the comrades who did so we had no grudge. On the contrary, we thought it quite right that those who had no capacity for mathematics or no memory for geography, should improve their total of marks by ordering from a draughtsman a drawing or a topographical map for which they would get 'a full twelve.' Only for the first two pupils of the form it would not have been fair to resort to such means, while the remainder could do it with untroubled consciences. But the teacher had no business to make drawings to order; and if he chose to act in this way, he ought to bear with resignation the noise and the tricks of his pupils. These were our ethics. Instead of this, no lesson passed without his lodging complaints, and each time he grew more arrogant.

As soon as we were moved to the fourth form, and felt ourselves naturalized citizens of the corps, we decided to tighten the bridle upon him. 'It is your own fault,' our elder comrades told us, ' that he takes such airs with you ; *we* used to keep him in obedience.' So we decided to bring him into subjection.

One day, two excellent comrades of our form

approached Ganz with cigarettes in their mouths, and asked him to oblige them with a light. Of course, that was only meant for a joke—no one ever thought of smoking in the class-rooms—and, according to our rules of propriety, Ganz had merely to send the two boys away; but he inscribed them in the journal, and they were severely punished. That was the last drop. We decided to give him a 'benefit night.' That meant that one day all the form, provided with rulers borrowed from the upper forms, would start an outrageous noise by striking the rulers against the tables, and send the teacher out of the class. However, the plot offered many difficulties. We had in our form a lot of 'goody' boys who would promise to join in the demonstration, but at the last moment would grow nervous and draw back, and then the teacher would name the others. In such enterprises unanimity is the first requisite, because the punishment, whatsoever it may be, is always lighter when it falls on the whole class instead of on a few.

The difficulties were overcome with a truly Machiavellian craft. At a given signal all were to turn their backs to Ganz, and then, with the rulers laid in readiness on the desks of the next row, they would produce the required noise. In this way the goody boys would not feel terrified at Ganz staring at them. But the signal? Whistling, as in robbers' tales, shouting, or even sneezing would not do: Ganz would be capable of naming anyone of us as having whistled or sneezed. The signal must be a silent one. One of us who drew nicely, would take his drawing to show it to Ganz, and the moment he returned and took his seat—that was to be the time!

All went on admirably.   Nesádoff took up his drawing, and Ganz corrected it in a few minutes, which
seemed to us an eternity.   He returned at last to his
seat ; he stopped for a moment, looking at us, he sat
down. . . .   All the form turned suddenly on their seats,
and the rulers rattled merrily within the desks, while
some of us shouted amidst the noise, ' Ganz out !
Down with him ! '   The noise was deafening ; all the
forms knew that Ganz had got his benefit night.   He
stood there, murmuring something, and finally went
out.   An officer ran in—the noise continued ; then the
sub-inspector dashed in, and after him the inspector.
The noise stopped.   Scolding began.

' The elder under arrest, at once ! ' the inspector
commanded ; and I, who was the first in the form, and
consequently the elder, was marched to the black cell.
That spared me seeing what followed.   The director
came ; Ganz was asked to name the ringleaders, but he
could name nobody.   ' They all turned their backs to
me, and began the noise,' was his reply.   Thereupon
the form was taken downstairs, and although flogging
had been completely abandoned in our school, this time
the two who had been reported because they asked for
a light were flogged with the birch rod, under the
pretext that the benefit night was a revenge for their
punishment.

I learned this ten days later, when I was allowed
to return to the class.   My name, which had been
inscribed on the red board in the class, was wiped off.
To this I was indifferent ; but I must confess that
the ten days in the cell, without books, seemed to me
rather long, so that I composed (in horrible verses) a

poem, in which the deeds of the fourth form were duly glorified.

Of course our form became now the heroes of the school. For a month or so we had to tell and retell all about the affair to the other forms, and received congratulations for having managed it with such unanimity that nobody was caught separately. And then came the Sundays—all the Sundays down to Christmas—that the form had to remain at the school, not being allowed to go home. Being all kept together, we managed to make those Sundays very gay. The mammas of the goody boys brought them heaps of sweets; those who had some money spent it in buying mountains of pastry— substantial before dinner, and sweet after it—while in the evenings the friends from the other forms smuggled in quantities of fruit for the brave fourth form.

Ganz gave up inscribing anyone; but drawing was totally lost for us. No one wanted to learn drawing from that mercenary man.

III

My brother Alexander was at that time at Moscow, in a corps of cadets, and we maintained a lively correspondence. As long as I stayed at home this was impossible, because our father considered it his prerogative to read all letters addressed to our house, and he would soon have put an end to any but a commonplace correspondence. Now we were free to discuss in our letters whatever we liked. The only difficulty was to get money for stamps ; but we soon learned to write in so small a hand that we could convey an incredible amount of matter in each letter. Alexander, whose handwriting was beautiful, contrived to get four printed pages on one single page of notepaper, and his microscopic lines were as legible as the best small type print. It is a pity that these letters, which he kept as precious relics, have disappeared. The State police, during one of their raids, robbed him even of these treasures.

Our first letters were mostly about the little details of my new surroundings, but our correspondence soon took a more serious character. My brother could not write about trifles. Even in society he became animated only when some serious discussion was engaged in, and complained of feeling 'a dull pain in the brain '—a physical pain, as he used to say—when he was with people who cared only for small talk. He was very much in advance of me in his intellectual development and he urged me forward, raising new scientific and philosophical questions one after another, and advising me what to read or to study. What a happiness it was for me to have such a brother !—a brother who, moreover, loved me passionately. To him I owe the best part of my development.

Sometimes he would advise me to read poetry, and would send me in his letters quantities of verses and whole poems, which he wrote from memory. ' Read poetry,' he wrote : ' poetry makes men better.' How often, in my after life, I realized the truth of this remark of his! Read poetry : it makes men better!

He himself was a poet, and had a wonderful facility for
writing most musical verses; indeed, I think it a great
pity that he abandoned poetry.   But the reaction
against art, which arose among the Russian youth in
the early sixties, and which Turguéneff has depicted in
'Bazároff' (*Fathers and Sons*), induced him to look
upon his verses with contempt, and to plunge headlong
into the natural sciences.   I must say, however, that my
favourite poet was none of those whom his poetical gift,
his musical ear, and his philosophical turn of mind
made him like best.   His favourite Russian poet was
Venevítinoff, while mine was Nekrásoff, whose verses
were very often unmusical, but appealed most to my
heart by their sympathy for 'the downtrodden and ill-
treated.'

'One must have a set purpose in his life,' he wrote
me once.   'Without an aim, without a purpose, life is
not life.'   And he advised me to get a purpose in my
life worth living for.   I was too young then to find one;
but something undetermined, vague, 'good' altogether,
already rose under that appeal, even though I could not
say what that 'good' would be.

Our father gave us very little spending money, and
I never had any to buy a single book; but if Alexander
got a few roubles from some aunt, he never spent a penny
of it for pleasure, but bought a book and sent it to me.
He objected, though, to indiscriminate reading.   'One
must have some question,' he wrote, 'addressed to the
book one is going to read.'   However, I did not then
appreciate this remark, and cannot think now without
amazement of the number of books, often of a quite
special character, which I read, in all branches, but

particularly in the domain of history. I did not waste my time upon French novels, since Alexander, years before, had characterized them in one blunt sentence : ‘ They are stupid and full of bad language.’

The great questions concerning the conception we should form of the universe—our *Weltanschauung*, as the Germans say—were, of course, the dominant subjects in our correspondence. In our childhood we had never been religious. We were taken to church ; but in a Russian church, in a small parish or in a village, the solemn attitude of the people is far more impressive than the Mass itself. Of all that I ever had heard in church only two things had impressed me : the twelve passages from the Gospels, relative to the sufferings of the Christ, which are read in Russia at the night service on the eve of Good Friday, and the short prayer condemning the spirit of domination, which is recited during the Great Lent, and is really beautiful by reason of its simple, unpretentious words and feeling. Púshkin has rendered it into Russian verse.

Later on, at St. Petersburg, I went several times to a Roman Catholic church, but the theatrical character of the service and the absence of real feeling in it shocked me, the more so when I saw there with what simple faith some retired Polish soldier or a peasant woman would pray in a remote corner. I also went to a Protestant church ; but coming out of it I caught myself murmuring Goethe’s words :—

> But you will never link hearts together
> Unless the linking springs from your own heart.

Alexander, in the meantime, had embraced with his usual passion the Lutheran faith. He had read Michelet's book on Servetus, and had worked out for himself a religion on the lines of that great fighter. He studied with enthusiasm the Augsburg declaration, which he copied out and sent me, and our letters now became full of discussions about grace, and of texts from the apostles Paul and James. I followed my brother, but theological discussions did not deeply interest me. Since I had recovered from the typhoid fever I had taken to quite different reading.

Our sister Hélène, who was now married, was at St. Petersburg, and every Saturday night I went to visit her. Her husband had a good library, in which the French philosophers of the last century and the modern French historians were well represented, and I plunged into them. Such books were prohibited in Russia, and evidently could not be taken to school; so I spent most of the night, every Saturday, in reading the works of the encyclopædists, the 'Philosophical Dictionary' of Voltaire, the writings of the Stoics, especially Marcus Aurelius, and so on. The infinite immensity of the universe, the greatness of nature, its poetry, its ever throbbing life, impressed me more and more; and that never-ceasing life and its harmonies gave me the ecstasy of admiration which the young soul thirsts for, while my favourite poets supplied me with an expression in words of that awakening love of mankind and faith in its progress which make the best part of youth and impress man for a life.

Alexander, by this time, had gradually come to a Kantian agnosticism, and the 'relativity of perceptions,'

'perceptions in time and space, and time only,' and so on, filled pages and pages in our letters, the writing of which became more and more microscopical as the subjects under discussion grew in importance. But neither then nor later on, when we used to spend hours and hours in discussing Kant's philosophy, could my brother convert me to become a disciple of the Königsberg philosopher.

Natural sciences—that is, mathematics, physics, and astronomy—were my chief studies. In the year 1858, before Darwin had brought out his immortal work, a professor of zoology at the Moscow University, Roulier, published three lectures on transformism, and my brother took up at once his ideas concerning the variability of species. He was not satisfied, however, with approximate proofs only, and began to study a number of special books on heredity and the like, communicating to me in his letters the main facts, as well as his ideas and his doubts. The appearance of the 'Origin of Species' did not settle his doubts on several special points, but only raised new questions and gave him the impulse for further studies. We afterward discussed—and that discussion lasted for many years—various questions relative to the origin of variations, their chances of being transmitted and being accentuated; in short, those questions which have been raised quite lately in the Weismann-Spencer controversy, in Galton's researches, and in the works of the modern Neo-Lamarckians. Owing to his philosophical and critical mind, Alexander had noticed at once the fundamental importance of these questions for the theory of variability of species, even though they were so often overlooked then by many naturalists.

I must also mention a temporary excursion into the domain of political economy. In the years 1858 and 1859 everyone in Russia spoke of political economy; lectures on free trade and protective duties attracted crowds of people, and my brother, who was not yet absorbed by the variability of species, took a lively though temporary interest in economical matters, sending me for reading the 'Political Economy' of Jean Baptiste Say. I read a few chapters only: tariffs and banking operations did not interest me in the least; but Alexander took up these matters so passionately that he even wrote letters to our stepmother, trying to interest her in the intricacies of the customs duties. Later on, in Siberia, as we were re-reading some of the letters of that period, we laughed like children when we fell upon one of his epistles in which he complained of our stepmother's incapacity to be moved even by such burning questions, and raged against a green-grocer whom he had caught in the street, and who, 'would you believe it,' he wrote with signs of exclamation, 'although he was a tradesman, affected a pig-headed indifference to tariff questions!'

Every summer about one-half of the pages were taken to a camp at Peterhof. The lower forms, how-ever were dispensed from joining the camp, and I spent the first two summers at Nikólskoye. To leave the school, to take the train to Moscow, and there to meet Alexander was such a happy prospect that I used to count the days that had to pass till that glorious one should arrive. But on one occasion a great disappointment awaited me at Moscow. Alexander had not passed his examinations, and was left for another year in the same form. He was, in fact, too young to enter the special classes ; but our father was very angry with him, nevertheless, and would not permit us to see each other. I felt very sad. We were not children any more, and had so much to say to each other. I tried to obtain permission to go to our aunt Sulíma, at whose house I might meet Alexander, but it was absolutely refused. After our father re-married we were never allowed to see our mother's relations.

That spring our Moscow house was full of guests. Every night the reception-rooms were flooded with lights, the band played, the confectioner was busy making ices and pastry, and card-playing went on in the great hall till a late hour. I strolled aimlessly about in the brilliantly illuminated rooms, and felt unhappy.

One night, after ten, a servant beckoned me, telling me to come out to the entrance hall. I went. 'Come to the coachmen's house,' the old major-domo Frol whispered to me. 'Alexander Alexéievich is here.'

I dashed across the yard, up the flight of steps leading to the coachmen's house, and into a wide, half-dark room, where, at the immense dining-table of the servants, I saw Alexander.

'Sásha, dear, how did you come ? ' and in a moment we rushed into each other's arms, hugging each other and unable to speak from emotion.

'Hush, hush ! they may overhear you,' said the servants' cook, Praskóvia, wiping away her tears with her apron. 'Poor orphans ! If your mother were only alive———'

Old Frol stood, his head deeply bent, his eyes also twinkling.

'Look here, Pétya, not a word to anyone; to no one,' he said, while Praskóvia placed on the table an earthenware jar full of porridge for Alexander.

He, glowing with health, in his cadet uniform, already had begun to talk about all sorts of matters, while he rapidly emptied the porridge pot. I could hardly make him tell me how he came there at such a late hour. We lived then near the Smolénsky boulevard, within a stone's throw of the house where our mother died, and the corps of cadets was at the opposite out-skirts of Moscow, full five miles away.

He had made a doll out of bedclothes, and had put it in his bed, under the blankets ; then he went to the tower, descended from a window, came out unnoticed, and walked the whole distance.

'Were you not afraid at night in the deserted fields round your córps ? ' I asked.

'What had I to fear ? Only lots of dogs were upon me ; I had teased them myself. To-morrow I shall take my sword with me.'

The coachmen and other servants came in and out ; they sighed as they looked at us, and took seats at a dis-tance, along the walls, exchanging words in a subdued tone so as not to disturb us ; while we two, in each other's arms, sat there till midnight, talking about nebulæ and Laplace's hypothesis, the structure of matter, the struggles of the papacy under Boniface VIII. with the imperial power, and so on.

From time to time one of the servants would hurriedly run in, saying, ' Pétinka, go and show thyself in
the hall ; they may ask for thee.'

I implored Sásha not to come next night ; but he
came, nevertheless—not without having had a scrimmage
with the dogs, against whom he had taken his sword.
I responded with feverish haste, when, earlier than the
day before, I was called once more to the coachmen's
house. Alexander had made part of the journey in a
cab. The previous night, one of the servants had
brought him what he had got from the card-players
and asked him to take it. He took some small coin to
hire a cab, and so he came earlier than on his first visit.

He intended to come next night, too, but for some
reason it would have been dangerous for the servants,
and we decided to part till the autumn. A short ' official '
note made me understand next day that his nocturnal
escapades had passed unnoticed. How terrible would
have been the punishment, if they had been discovered.
It is awful to think of it : flogging before the corps till
he was carried away unconscious on a sheet, and then
degradation to a soldiers' sons' battalion—anything was
possible, in those times.

What our servants would have suffered for hiding
us, if information of the affair had reached our father's
ears, would have been equally terrible ; but they knew
how to keep secrets and not to betray one another.
They all knew of the visits of Alexander, but none of
them whispered a word to anyone of the family. They
and I were the only ones in the house who ever knew
anything about it.

IV

THAT same year I made my first start as an explorer of
popular life, and this little work brought me one step
nearer to our peasants, making me see them under a new
light ; it also helped me later on a great deal in Siberia.

Every year, in July, on the day of ' the Holy Virgin
of Kazán ' which was the fête of our church, a pretty
large fair was held in Nikólskoye. Tradesmen came
from the neighbouring towns, and many thousands of
peasants flocked from thirty miles round to our village,
which for a couple of days had a most animated aspect.
A remarkable description of the village fairs of South
Russia had just been published that year by the Slavophile Aksákoff, and my brother, who was then at the
height of his politico-economical enthusiasm, advised
me to make a statistical description of our fair, and to
determine the return of goods brought in and sold. I
followed his advice, and to my great amazement I really
succeeded : my estimate of returns, so far as I can judge
now, was not more unreliable than many similar estimates in books of statistics.

Our fair lasted only a little more than twenty-four
hours. On the eve of the fête, the great open space given
to it was full of life and animation. Long rows of stalls,
to be used for the sale of cottons, ribbons, and all sorts of
peasant women's attire, were hurriedly built. The
restaurant, a substantial stone building, was furnished
with tables, chairs and benches, and its floor was strewn
over with bright yellow sand. Three wine-shops were

erected in three different places, and freshly cut brooms, planted on high poles, rose high in the air to attract the peasants from a distance.   Rows and rows of light shops for the sale of crockery, boots, stoneware, ginger-bread, and all sorts of small things, rose as if by a magic wand ; while in a special corner holes were dug in the ground to receive immense cauldrons in which bushels of millet and sarrasin and whole sheep were boiled, for supplying the thousands of visitors with hot *schi* and *kásha* (soup and porridge).   In the afternoon, the four roads leading to the fair were blocked by hundreds of peasant carts, and cattle, corn, casks filled with tar, and heaps of pottery were exhibited along the roadsides.

The night service on the eve of the fête was performed in our church with great solemnity.   Half a dozen priests and deacons from the neighbouring villages took part in it, and their chanters, reinforced by young tradespeople, sang in the choir with such ritornellos as could only be heard at the bishop's in Kalúga.   The church was crowded ; all prayed fervently.   The tradespeople vied with each other in the number and sizes of the wax candles which they lighted before the ikons, as offerings to the local saints for the success of their trade ; and the crowd being so thick as not to allow the last comers to reach the altar, candles of all sizes—thick and thin, white and yellow, according to the offerer's wealth—were transmitted from the back of the church through the crowd, with whispers : 'To the Holy Virgin of Kazán, our Protector,' 'To Nicholas the Favourite,' 'To Frol and Laur ' (the horse saints—that was from those who had horses to sell), or simply to ' the Saints ' without a further specification.

Immediately after the night service was over, the 'fore-fair' began, and I had now to plunge headlong into my work of asking hundreds of people what was the value of the goods they had brought in. To my great astonishment my task went on admirably. Of course, I was myself asked questions: 'Why do you do this?' 'Is it not for the old prince, who intends increasing the market dues?' But the assurance that the 'old prince' knew and would know nothing of it (he would have found it a disgraceful occupation) settled all doubts at once. I soon caught the proper way of asking questions, and after I had taken half a dozen cups of tea in the restaurant with some trades-people (oh, horror, if my father had learned that!), all went on very well. Vasíly Ivánoff, the elder of Nikólskoye, a beautiful young peasant with a fine intelligent face and a silky fair beard, took an interest in my work. 'Well, if thou wantest it for thy learning, get at it; thou wilt tell us later on what thou hast found out '—was his conclusion, and he told some of the people that it was 'all right.' Everyone knew him for miles round, and the word passed round the fair that no harm would ensue to the peasants by giving me the information.

In short, the 'imports' were determined very nicely. But next day, the 'sales' offered certain diffi-culties, chiefly with the dry goods' merchants, who did not themselves yet know how much they had sold. On the day of the fête the young peasant women simply stormed the shops, each of them having sold some linen of her own making and now buying some cotton print for a dress and a bright kerchief for herself, a coloured handkerchief for her husband, perhaps some neck lace, a ribbon or two, and a number of small gifts to grandmother, grandfather, and the children who had remained at home.   As to the peasants who sold crockery, or ginger-cakes, or cattle and hemp, they at once determined their sales, especially the old women. 'Good sale, grandmother?' I would ask. 'No need to complain, my son. Why should I anger God? Nearly all is sold.'   And out of their small items the tens of thousand roubles grew in my note-book. One point only remained unsettled.   A wide space was given up to many hundreds of peasant women who stood in the burning sun, each with her piece of handwoven linen, sometimes exquisitely fine, which she had brought for sale—scores of buyers, with gypsy faces and shark-like looks, moving about in the crowd and buying.   Only rough estimates of these sales could evidently be made.   •

I made no reflections at that time about this new experience of mine ; I was simply happy to see that it was not a failure.   But the serious good sense and sound judgment of the Russian peasants which I witnessed during this couple of days, left upon me a lasting impression.   Later on, when we were making socialist propaganda among the peasants, I could not but wonder why some of my friends, who had received a seemingly far more democratic education than myself, did not know how to talk to the peasants or to the factory workers from the country.   They tried to imitate the 'peasants' talk,' by introducing into it lots of so-called 'popular phrases' and only rendered it the more incomprehensible.

Nothing of the sort is needed, either in talking to peasants or in writing for them. The Great Russian peasant perfectly well understands the educated man's talk, provided that it is not stuffed with words taken from foreign languages. What the peasant does not understand is abstract notions when they are not illustrated by concrete examples. But when you speak to the Russian peasant plainly, and start from concrete facts—and the same is true with regard to village-folk of all nationalities—my experience is that there is no generalization from the whole world of science, social or natural, which could not be conveyed to the averagely intelligent man if you yourself understand it concretely. The chief difference between the educated and the uneducated man is, I should say, in the latter not being able to follow a chain of conclusions. He grasps the first of them, and may be the second, but he gets tired at the third, if he does not see what you are driving at. But, how often do we meet with the same difficulty in educated people !

One more impression I gathered from that work of my boyhood—an impression which I formulated but later on, and which will probably astonish many a reader. It is the spirit of equality which is highly developed in the Russian peasant and, in fact, in the rural population everywhere. The Russian peasant is capable of much servile obedience to the landlord or to the police officer ; he will bend before their will in a servile manner ; but he does not consider them superior men, and if the next moment that same landlord or officer talks to the same peasant about hay or ducks, the latter will converse with them as an equal to an equal.   I never saw in a Russian peasant that servility, grown to be a second nature, with which a small functionary talks to a highly placed one, or a valet to his master.   The peasant much too easily submits to force, but he does not worship it.

I returned that summer from Nikólskoye to Moscow in a new fashion.   There being then no railway between Kalúga and Moscow, a man, Buck by name, kept some sort of carriages running between the two towns.   Our people never thought of travelling in such a way : they had their own horses and conveyances ; but when my father, in order to save my step-mother a double journey, offered me, half in joke, to travel alone in that way, I accepted his offer with delight.

An old and very stout tradesman's wife and myself on the back seats, and a small tradesman or artisan on the front seat, were the only occupants of the carriage.   I found the journey very pleasant—first of all because I travelled by myself (I was not yet sixteen), and next because the old lady, who had brought with her for a three days' journey a colossal hamper full of provisions, treated me to all sorts of home-made delicacies.   All the surroundings during that journey were delightful.   One evening especially is still vivid in my memory.   We came at night to one of the great villages and stopped at some inn.   The old lady ordered a samovár for herself, while I went out in the street, walking about anywhere.   A small 'white inn' at which only food is served, but no drinks, attracted my attention and I went in.   Numbers of peasants sat round the small tables, covered with white napkins, and enjoyed their tea. I did the same.

All was so new for me in these surroundings. It was a village of 'Crown peasants'—that is, peasants who had not been serfs and enjoyed a relative well-being, probably owing to the weaving of linen which they carried on as a home industry. Slow, serious conversations, with occasional laughter, were going on at those tables, and after the usual introductory questions, I soon found myself engaged in a conversation with a dozen peasants about the crops in our neighbourhood, and answering all sorts of questions. They wanted to know all about St. Petersburg, and most of all about the rumours concerning the coming abolition of serfdom. And a feeling of simplicity and of the natural relations of equality, as well as of hearty good-will, which I always felt afterwards when among peasants or in their houses, took possession of me at that inn. Nothing extraordinary happened that night, so that I even ask myself if the incident is worth mentioning at all; and yet that warm, dark night in the village, that small inn, that talk with the peasants, and the keen interest they took in hundreds of things lying far beyond their habitual surroundings, have made ever since a poor 'white inn' more attractive to me than the best restaurant in the world.

V

STORMY times came now in the life of our corps. When
Girardot was dismissed, his place was taken by one of
our officers, Captain B——. He was rather good-
natured than otherwise, but he had got into his head
that he was not treated by us with due reverence,
corresponding to the high position which he now
occupied, and he tried to enforce upon us more respect
and awe toward himself. He began by quarrelling
about all sorts of petty things with the upper form,
and—what was still worse—he attempted to destroy
our 'liberties,' the origin of which was lost in the
darkness of time and which, insignificant in themselves,
were perhaps on that same account only the dearer
to us.

The result of it was that the school broke for several
days into an open revolt, which ended in wholesale
punishment, and the exclusion from the corps of two
of our favourite pages de chambre.

Then, the same captain began to intrude in the
class-rooms, where we used to spend one hour in the
morning in preparing our lessons before the classes
began. We were considered to be there under our
teaching staff, and were happy to have nothing to do
with our military chiefs. We resented that intrusion
very much, and one day I loudly expressed our discontent, saying to the captain that this was the place
of the inspector of the classes, not his. I spent weeks
under arrest for that frankness, and perhaps should

have been excluded from the school, were it not that
the inspector of the classes, his assistant, and even our
old director, judged that after all I had only expressed
aloud what they all used to say to themselves.

No sooner all these troubles were over, than
the death of the Dowager-Empress—the widow of
Nicholas I.—brought a new interruption in our work.

The burial of crowned heads is always so arranged
as to produce a deep impression on the crowds, and it
must be owned that this object is attained.   The body
of the empress was brought from Tsárkoye Seló, where
she died, to St. Petersburg, and here, followed by the
imperial family, all the high dignitaries of the state,
and scores of thousands of functionaries and corporations, and preceded by hundreds of clergy and choirs,
it was taken from the railway station through the
main thoroughfares to the fortress, where it had to lie
in state for several weeks.   A hundred thousand men of
the Guard were placed along the streets, and thousands
of people, dressed in the most gorgeous uniforms,
preceded, accompanied, and followed the hearse in a
solemn procession.   Litanies were sung at every
important crossing of the streets, and here the ringing
of the bells on the church towers, the voices of vast
choirs, and the sounds of the military bands united in
the most impressive way, so as to make people believe
that the immense crowds really mourned the loss of
the empress.

As long as the body lay in state in the cathedral of
the fortress, the pages, among others, had to keep the
watch round it, night and day.   Three pages de
chambre and three maids of honour always stood close

by the coffin, placed on a high pedestal, while some
twenty pages were stationed on the platform upon
which litanies were sung twice every day, in the
presence of the emperor and all his family.   Consequently, every week nearly one-half of the corps was
taken in turns to the fortress, to lodge there.   We
were relieved every two hours, and in the daytime our
service was not difficult; but when we had to rise in
the night, to dress in our court uniforms, and then to
walk through the dark and gloomy inner courts of the
fortress to the cathedral, to the sound of the gloomy
chime of the fortress bells, a cold shiver seized me at
the thought of the prisoners who were immured somewhere in this Russian Bastille.   'Who knows,' thought
I, 'whether in my turn I shall not also have to join
them one day or other?'

The burial did not pass without an accident which
might have had serious consequences.   An immense
canopy had been erected under the dome of the cathedral over the coffin.   A huge gilded crown rose above
it, and from this crown an immense purple mantle
lined with ermine hung towards the four thick pilasters which support the dome of the cathedral.   It was
impressive, but we boys soon made out that the crown
was made of gilded cardboard and wood, the mantle
was of velvet only in its lower part, while higher up it
was red cotton, and that the ermine lining was simply
cotton flannelette or swandown to which black tails
of squirrels had been sewn, while the escutcheons
which represented the arms of Russia, veiled with
black crêpe, were simple cardboard.   But the crowds
which were allowed at certain hours of the night to

pass by the coffin, and to kiss in a hurry the gold brocade which covered it, surely had no time to closely examine the flannelette ermine or the cardboard escutcheons, and the desired theatrical effect was obtained even by such cheap means.

When a litany is sung in Russia all the people present hold lighted wax candles, which have to be put out after certain prayers have been read. The Imperial family also held such candles, and one day the young son of the grand duke Constantine, seeing that the others put out their candles by turning them upside down, did the same. The black gauze which hung behind him from an escutcheon took fire, and in a second the escutcheon and the cotton stuff were ablaze. An immense tongue of fire ran up the heavy folds of the supposed ermine mantle.

The service was stopped. All looks were directed with terror towards the tongue of fire, which went higher and higher towards the cardboard crown and the wood_work which supported the whole structure. Bits of burning stuff began to fall down, threatening to set fire to the black gauze veils of the ladies present.

Alexander II. lost his presence of mind for a couple of seconds only, but he recovered immediately and said in a composed voice: ' The coffin must be taken ! ' The pages de chambre at once covered it with the thick gold brocade, and we all advanced to lift the heavy coffin ; but in the meantime the big tongue of flame had broken into a number of smaller ones, which now slowly devoured only the fluffy outside of the cotton stuff and, meeting more and more dust and soot in the upper part of the structure, gradually died out in the folds.

I cannot say what I looked most at : the creeping
fire or the stately slender figures of the three ladies who
stood by the coffin, the long trains of their black
dresses spreading over the steps which led to the upper
platform, and their black lace veils hanging down their
shoulders.   None of them had made the slightest movement : they stood like three beautiful carved images.
Only in the dark eyes of one of them, Mdlle. Gamaléya,
tears glittered like pearls.   She was a daughter of
South Russia, and was the only really handsome lady
amongst the maids of honour at the Court.

At the corps, in the meantime, everything was upside down.   The classes were interrupted ; those of us
who returned from the fortress were lodged in temporary
quarters, and, having nothing to do, spent the whole day
in all sorts of frolics.   In one of them we managed to
open a cupboard which stood in the room and contained
a splendid collection of models of all kinds of animals
for the teaching of natural history.   That was its
official purpose ; but it was never even so much as
shown to us, and now that we got hold of it we utilised
it in our own way.   With the human skull which made
part of the collection we made a ghostly figure where-
with to frighten at night other comrades and the officers.
As to the animals, we placed them in the most unappro-
priate positions and groups : monkeys were seen riding
on lions, sheep were playing with leopards, the giraffe
danced with the elephant, and so on.   The worst was
that a few days later one of the Prussian princes who
had come to assist at the burial ceremony (it was the
one, I think, who became later on the Emperor
Frederick) visited our school, and was shown all that

concerned our education. Our director did not fail to
boast of the excellent educational appliances which we
had at the school, and brought him to that same unfortunate cupboard. . . . When the German prince
caught a glimpse of our zoological classification, he
drew a long face and quickly turned away. Our old
director looked horrified; he had lost the power of speech,
and only pointed repeatedly with his hand at some star-
fishes which were placed in glass boxes on the walls
by the sides of the cupboard. The suite of the prince
tried to look as if they had noticed nothing, and only
threw rapid glimpses at the cause of so much disturbance, while we wicked boys made all sorts of faces in
order not to burst with laughter.

VI

THE school years of a Russian youth are so very
different from what they are in West European
schools that I must dwell upon my school life.
Russian youths, as a rule, while they are yet at a
lyceum or in a military school, already take an interest
in a wide circle of social, political, and philosophical
matters. It is true that the corps of pages was, of all
schools, the least congenial medium for such a development; but in those years of general revival, broader ideas
penetrated even into our midst and carried some of us
away, without, however, preventing us from taking a

very lively part in ' benefit nights ' and all sorts of frolics,

While I was in the fourth form I took an interest in history, and with the aid of notes made during the lessons—I knew that university students do it that way—and helping myself with reading, I wrote quite a course of early mediæval history for my own use. Next year the struggle between Pope Boniface VIII. and the Imperial power attracted my special attention, and now it became my ambition to gain admission to the Imperial library as a reader, in order thoroughly to study that great struggle. This was contrary to the rules of the library, pupils of secondary schools not being admitted; our good Herr Becker, however, smoothed the way out of the difficulty, and I was allowed one day to enter the sanctuary and to take a seat at one of the readers' small tables, on one of the red velvet sofas with which the reading-room was then furnished.

From various text-books and some books from our own library, I soon got to the sources. Knowing no Latin, I discovered nevertheless a rich supply of original sources in Old Teutonic and Old French, and found an immense æsthetic enjoyment in the quaint structure and expressiveness of the latter in the Chronicles. Quite a new structure of society and quite a world of complicated relations opened before me ; and from that time I learned to value far more the original sources of history than works in which it is generalized in accordance with modern views—the prejudices of modern politics, or even mere current formulæ being substituted for the real life of the period. Nothing gives more impetus to one's intellectual development than some sort of independent research, and these studies of mine immensely helped me afterwards.

Unhappily, I had to abandon them when we reached the second form (the last but one). The pages had to study during the last two years nearly all that was taught in other military schools in three 'special' forms, and we had an immense amount of work to do for the school. Natural sciences, mathematics, and military sciences necessarily relegated history to the background.

In the second form we began seriously to study physics. We had an excellent teacher—a very intelligent man with a sarcastic turn of mind, who hated learning from memory, and managed to make us *think* instead of merely learning facts. He was a good mathematician, and taught us physics on a mathematical basis, admirably explaining at the same time the leading ideas of physical research and physical apparatus. Some of his questions were so original and his explanations so good that they have engraved themselves for ever on my memory.

Our text-book of physics was pretty good (most text-books for the military schools had been written by the best men at the time), but it was rather old, and our teacher, who followed his own system in teaching, began to prepare a short summary of his lessons—a sort of *aide-mémoire*—for the use of our form. However, after a few weeks it so happened that the task of writing this summary fell upon me, and our teacher, acting as a true pedagogist, trusted it entirely to me, only reading the proofs. When we came to the chapters of heat, electricity, and magnetism, they had to be written entirely anew, and this I did,. thus preparing a nearly complete text-book of physics, which was printed for the use of the school.

- In the second form we also began to study chemistry, and we also had a first-rate teacher—a passionate lover of the subject who had himself made valuable original researches. The years 1859–61 were years of a universal revival of taste in the exact sciences : Grove, Clausius, Joule, and Séguin showed that heat and all physical forces are but divers modes of motion ; Helmholtz began about that time his epoch-making researches in sound ; and Tyndall, in his popular lectures, made one touch, so to say, the very atoms and molecules. Gerhardt and Avogadro introduced the theory of substitutions, and Mendeléeff, Lothar Meyer, and Newlands discovered the periodical law of elements ; Darwin, with his ' Origin of Species,' revolutionised all biological sciences ; while Karl Vogt and Moleschott, following Claude Bernard, laid the foundations of true psychology in physiology. It was a great time of scientific revival, and the current which directed men's minds towards natural science was irresistible. Numbers of excellent books were published at that time in Russian translations, and I soon understood that whatever one's subsequent studies might be, a thorough knowledge of the natural sciences and familiarity with their methods must lie at the foundation.

Five or six of us joined together to get some sort of laboratory for ourselves. With the elementary apparatus recommended for beginners in Stöckhardt's excellent text-book we started our laboratory in a small bedroom of two of our comrades, the brothers Zasétsky. Their father, an old retired admiral, was delighted to see his sons engaged in so useful a pursuit, and did not object to our coming together on Sundays and during the holidays in that room by the side of his own study. With Stöckhardt's book as a guide, we systematically made all experiments. I must say that once we nearly set the house on fire, and that more than once we poisoned all the rooms with chlorine and similar stuffs. But the old admiral, when we related the adventure at dinner time, took it very nicely, and told us how he and his comrades also nearly set a house on fire in the far less useful pursuit of punch making; while the mother only said, amidst her paroxysms of coughing : 'Of course, if it *is* necessary for your learning to handle such nasty smelling things, then there's nothing to be done ! '

After dinner she usually took her seat at the piano, and till late at night we would go on singing duos, trios, and choruses from the operas. Or else we would take the score of some Italian or Russian opera and go through it from the beginning to the end, recitatives and all—the mother and her daughter taking the parts of the *prime donne*, while we managed more or rather less successfully to maintain all other parts. Chemistry and music thus went hand in hand.

Higher mathematics also absorbed a great deal of my time. Four or five of us had already decided that we should not enter a regiment of the Guards, where

all our time would be given to military drill and
parades, and we intended to enter, after promotion,
one of the military academies—artillery or engineering.
In order to do so we had to prepare in higher geometry,
the differential and the beginnings of the integral
calculus, and we took private lessons for that purpose.
At the same time, elementary astronomy being taught
to us under the name of mathematical geography, I
plunged into astronomical reading, especially during
the last year of my stay at school. The never ceasing
life of the universe, which I conceived as *life* and
evolution, became for me an inexhaustible source of
higher poetical thought, and gradually the sense of
man's oneness with Nature, both animate and inanimate
—the poetry of Nature—became the philosophy of my
life.

If the teaching in our school were only limited to
the subjects I have mentioned, our time would already
be pretty well occupied. But we also had to study
in the domain of humanitarian science, history, law
(that is, the main outlines of the Russian Code), and
political economy in its essential leading principles,
including a course of comparative statistics ; and we
had to master formidable courses of military sciences :
tactics, military history (the campaigns of 1812 and
1815 in all their details), artillery, and field fortification.
Looking now back upon this education I think that
apart from the subjects relative to military warfare,
which might have been advantageously substituted by
more detailed studies in the exact sciences, the variety
of subjects which we were taught was not beyond the
capacities of the average youth. Owing to a pretty

good knowledge of elementary mathematics and physics, which we gained in the lower forms, nearly all of us managed to master all these subjects. Some subjects were neglected by most of us, especially law, as also modern history, for which we had unfortunately an old wreck of a master who was only kept at his post in order to give him his full old age pension. Moreover, some latitude was given to us in the choice of the subjects we liked best, and, while we underwent severe examinations in these chosen subjects, we were treated rather leniently in the remainder. But the chief cause of the relative success which was obtained in the school was that the teaching was rendered as concrete as possible. As soon as we had learned elementary geometry on paper, we re-learned it in the field with poles and the surveyor's chain, and next with the astrolabe, the compass, and the surveyor's table. After such a concrete training, elementary astronomy offered no difficulties, while the surveys themselves were an endless source of enjoyment.

The same system of concrete teaching was applied to fortification. In the winter we solved such problems as, for instance, the following: 'Having a thousand men and a fortnight at your disposal, build the strongest fortification you can build to protect that bridge for a retreating army;' and we hotly discussed our schemes with the teacher when he criticised them. In the summer we applied that knowledge in the field. To these practical and concrete exercises I entirely attribute the easiness with which most of us mastered such a variety of subjects at the age of seventeen and eighteen.

With all that, we had plenty of time for amusement. Our best time was when the examinations were over, and we had three or four weeks quite free before going to camp; or when we returned from the camp, and had another three weeks free before the beginning of the lessons. The few of us who remained then in the school were allowed, during the vacations, to go out just as we liked, always finding bed and food at the school. I worked then in the library, or visited the picture galleries of the Hermitage, studying one by one all the best pictures of each school separately; or I went to the different Crown factories and works of playing cards, cottons, iron, china and glass, which are open to the public. Or we went out rowing on the Nevá, spending the whole night on the river, sometimes in the Gulf of Finland with fishermen—a melancholy northern night, during which the morning dawn meets the afterglow of the setting sun, and a book can be read in the open air at midnight. For all this we found plenty of time.

Since those visits to the factories I took a liking to strong and perfect machinery. Seeing how a gigantic paw, coming out of a shanty, grasps a log floating in the Nevá, pulls it inside, and puts it under the saws which cut it into boards; or how a huge red hot iron bar is transformed into a rail after it has passed between two cylinders, I understood the poetry of machinery. In our present factories, machinery work is killing for the worker, because he becomes a lifelong servant to a given machine and never is anything else. But this is a matter of bad organization, and has nothing to do with the machine itself. Over-

work and lifelong monotony are equally bad whether
the work is done with the hand, with plain tools, or
with a machine. But, apart from these, I fully understand the pleasure that man can derive from the con-
sciousness of the might of his machine, the intelligent
character of its work, the gracefulness of its movements, and the correctness of what it is doing, and I
think that William Morris's hatred of machines only
proved that the conception of the machine's power and
gracefulness was missing in his great poetical genius.

Music also played a very great part in my development. From it I borrowed even greater joys and
enthusiasm than from poetry. The Russian opera
hardly existed in those times; but the Italian opera,
which had a number of first-rate stars in it, was the
most popular institution at St. Petersburg. When
the *prima donna* Bósio fell ill, thousands of people,
chiefly of the youth, stood till late at night at the door
of her hotel to get news of her. She was not beautiful, but was so much so when she sang that young
men madly in love with her could be counted by
the hundred; and when she died she had a burial
which no one before had ever had at St. Petersburg.
'All Petersburg' was then divided into two camps:
the admirers of the Italian opera and those of the
French stage, which already then was showing in germ
the putrid Offenbachian current which a few years
later infected all Europe. Our form was also divided,
half and half, between these two currents, and I
belonged to the former. We were not permitted to go
to the pit or to the balcony, while all the boxes in the
Italian opera were always taken months in advance

by subscription, and even transmitted in certain families as an hereditary possession. But we gained admission, on Saturday nights, to the passages in the uppermost gallery, and had to stand there on our legs in a Turkish bath atmosphere ; while to conceal our showy uniforms we used to wear, in that Turkish bath, our black overcoats, lined with wadding and with a fur collar, tightly buttoned. It is a wonder that none of us got pneumonia in this way, especially as we came out overheated with the ovations which we used to make to our favourite singers, and stood afterwards at the stage door to catch once more a glimpse of our favourites, and to cheer them. The Italian opera in those years was in some strange way intimately connected with the Radical movement, and the revolutionary recitatives in ' Wilhelm Tell ' and ' The Puritans ' were always met with stormy applause and vociferations which went straight to the heart of Alexander II. ; while in the sixth story galleries, in the smoking-room of the opera, and at the stage door the best part of the St. Petersburg youth came together in a common idealist worship of a noble art. All this may seem childish ; but many higher ideas and pure inspirations were kindled in us by this worship of our favourite artists.

VII

EVERY summer we went out camping at Peterhóf, with the other military schools of the St. Petersburg district. All things considered, our life there was very pleasant, and certainly was excellent for our health : we slept in spacious tents, we bathed in the sea, and spent all the six weeks in open-air exercise.

In military schools the main purpose of camp life was evidently military drill, which we all disliked very much, but the dulness of which was occasionally relieved by making us take part in manœuvres. One night, as we were already going to bed, Alexander II. aroused the camp by having the alert sounded. In a few minutes all the camp was alive— several thousand boys gathering round their colours, and the guns of the artillery school booming in the stillness of the night. All military Peterhóf was galloping to our camp, but, owing to some misunderstanding, the emperor remained on foot. Orderlies were sent in all directions to get a horse for him, but there was none, and he, not being a good rider, would not ride any horse but one of his own. Alexander II. was very angry, and freely ventilated his anger. ' Imbecile (durák), have I only one horse ? ' I heard him shout to an orderly who reported that his horse was in another camp.

What with the increasing darkness, the booming of the guns, and the rattling of the cavalry, we boys grew very much excited, and when Alexander ordered charging, our column charged straight upon him. Tightly packed in the ranks, with lowered bayonets, we must have had a menacing aspect, for I saw Alexander II. who was still on foot, clearing the way for the column in three formidable jumps. I understood then the meaning of a column which is marching in serried ranks under the excitement of the music and the march itself. There stood before us the emperor—our commander, whom we all venerated very much ; but I felt that in this moving mass not one page or cadet would have moved an inch aside, or stopped awhile, to make room for him. We were the marching column—he was but an obstacle —and the column would have marched over him. ' Why should he be in our way ? ' the pages said afterwards. Boys, rifle in hand, are even more terrible in such cases than old soldiers.

Next year, when we took part in the great manœuvres of the St. Petersburg garrison, I got an insight into the sidelights of warfare. For two days in succession we did nothing but march up and down on a space of some twenty miles, without having the slightest idea of what was going on round us or for what purpose we were marched. Cannon boomed now in our neighbourhood and now far away : sharp musketry fire was heard somewhere in the hills and the woods ; orderlies galloped up and down bringing the order to advance and next the order to retreat—and we marched, marched, and marched, seeing no sense in all these movements and counter-movements. Masses of cavalry had passed along the same road, making out of it a deep mass of movable sand ; and we had to advance and retreat several times along the same road, till at last our column broke all discipline and represented an incoherent mass of pilgrims rather than a military unit.   The colours alone remained in the road ; the remainder slowly paced along the sides of the road, in the wood.   The orders and the supplications of the officers were of no avail.

Suddenly a shout came from behind : 'The emperor is coming !   The emperor !'   The officers ran about supplicating us to gather in the ranks : no one listened to them.

The emperor came and ordered to retreat once more —'Turn round !' the words of command resounded. 'The emperor is behind us, please turn round,' the officers whispered ; but the battalion hardly took any notice of the command, and none whatever of the presence of the emperor.   Happily, Alexander II. was no fanatic of militarism, and, after having said a few words to cheer us with a promise of rest, he galloped off.

I understood then how much depends in warfare upon the state of mind of the troops, and how little can be done by mere discipline when more than an average effort is required from the soldiers.   What can discipline do when tired troops have to make a supreme effort to reach the field of battle at a given hour ?   It is absolutely powerless. Only enthusiasm and confidence can at such moments induce the soldiers to do 'the impossible '—and it is the impossible that continually must be accomplished to secure success.   How often, later on in Siberia, I recalled to memory that object lesson when we also had to do the impossible during our scientific expeditions !

Comparatively little of our time was, however, given during our stay in the camp to military drill and manœuvres. A good deal of it was given to practical exercises in surveys and fortification. After a few preliminary exercises we were given a reflecting compass and told : ' Go and make a plan of, say, this lake or those roads, or that park, measuring the angles with the compass and the distances with your pace.' And early in the morning, after a hurriedly swallowed breakfast, the boy would fill his spacious military pockets with slices of rye bread, and would go out for four or five hours every day in the parks, miles away, mapping with his compass and paces the beautiful shady roads, the rivulets, and the lakes. His work was later on compared with accurate maps, and prizes in optical and drawing instruments at the boy's choice were awarded. For me these surveys were a deep source of enjoyment. That independent work, that isolation under the centuries-old trees, that life of the forest which I could enjoy undisturbed, while there was at the same time the interest in the work—all these left deep traces in my mind ; and if I later on became an explorer of Siberia and several of my comrades became explorers in Central Asia, the ground for it was prepared in these surveys.

And finally, in the last form, parties of four boys were taken every second day to some villages at a considerable distance from the camp, and there they had to make a detailed survey of several square miles with the aid of the surveyor's table and a telescopic ruler. Officers of the General Staff came from time to time to verify their work and to advise them. This life amidst the peasants in the villages had the best effect upon the intellectual and moral development of many boys.

At the same time, exercises were made in the construction of natural sized cross-sections of fortifications. We were taken out by an officer in the open field, and there we had to make the cross-sections of a bastion, or of a bridge head, nailing poles and battens together in exactly the same way as railway engineers do in tracing a railway. When it came to embrasures and barbettes, we had to calculate a great deal to obtain the inclinations of the different planes, and after that geometry in the space ceased to be difficult to understand.

We delighted in such work, and once, in town, finding in our garden a heap of clay and gravel, we at once began to build a real fortification on a reduced scale, with well calculated straight and oblique embrasures and barbettes. All was done very neatly, and our ambition now was to obtain some planks for making the platforms for the guns, and to place upon them the model guns which we had in our class-rooms.

But, alas, our trousers wore an alarming aspect. 'What are you doing there?' our captain exclaimed. 'Look at yourselves! You look like navvies' (that was exactly what we were proud of). 'What if the Grand Duke comes and finds you in such a state!'

'We will show him our fortifications and ask him to get us tools and boards for the platforms.'

All protests were vain. A dozen workers were sent next day to cart away our beautiful work, as if it were a mere heap of mud!

I mention this to show how children and youths long for real applications of what they learn at school

in abstract, and how stupid are the educators who are
unable to see what a powerful aid they could find in
concrete applications for helping their pupils to grasp
the real sense of the things they learn.

In our school all was directed towards training us
for warfare.   But we should have worked with the same
enthusiasm at tracing a railway, at building a log-house,
or at cultivating a garden or a field.   But all this long-
ing of the children and youths for *real* work is wasted
simply because our idea of the school is still the mediæval scholasticism, the mediæval monastery !

VIII

THE years 1857-61 were years of rich growth in the
intellectual forces of Russia.   All that had been whispered for the last decade, in the secrecy of friendly
meetings, by the generation represented in Russian
literature by Turguéneff, Tolstóy, Hérzen, Bakúnin,
Ogaryóff, Kavélin, Dostoévsky, Grigoróvich, Ostróvsky,
and Nekrásoff, began now to leak out in the press.
Censorship was still very rigorous ; but what could not
be said openly in political articles was smuggled in under
the form of novels, humorous sketches, or veiled com-
ments on West European events, and everyone read
between the lines and understood.

Having no acquaintances at St. Petersburg apart
from the school and a narrow circle of relatives, I stood
outside the radical movement of those years—miles,

in fact, away from it.   And yet this was, perhaps, the
main feature of the movement—that it had the power
to penetrate into so 'well meaning' a school as our
corps was, and to find an echo in such a circle as that
of my Moscow relatives.

I used at that time to spend my Sundays and holidays at the house of my aunt, mentioned in a previous
chapter under the name of Princess Mírski.   Prince
Mírski thought only of extraordinary lunches and
dinners, while his wife and their young daughter led a
very gay life.   My cousin was a beautiful girl of nineteen, of a most amiable disposition, and nearly all her
male cousins were madly in love with her.   She, in turn,
fell in love with one of them, and wanted to marry
him.   But to marry a cousin is considered a great sin
by the Russian Church, and the old princess tried in
vain to obtain a special permission from the high eccle-
siastical dignitaries.   Now she brought her daughter to
St. Petersburg, hoping that she might choose among
her many admirers a more suitable husband than her
own cousin.   It was labour lost, I must add; but their
fashionable apartment was full of brilliant young men
from the Guards and from the diplomatic service.

Such a house would be the last to be thought of in
connection with revolutionary ideas; and yet it was in
that house that I made my first acquaintance with the
revolutionary literature of the times.   The great refugee,
Hérzen, had just begun to issue at London his review,
'The Polar Star,' which made a commotion in Russia,
even in the palace circles, and was widely circulated
secretly at St. Petersburg.   My cousin got it in some
way, and we used to read it together.   Her heart

revolted against the obstacles which were put in the way
of her happiness, and her mind was the more open to
the powerful criticisms which the great writer launched
against the Russian autocracy and all the rotten system
of misgovernment. With a feeling near to worship I
used to look on the medallion which was printed on the
paper cover of ' The Polar Star,' and which represented
the noble heads of the five ' Decembrists ' whom
Nicholas I. had hanged after the rebellion of Decem-
ber 14, 1825—Bestúzheff, Kahóvskiy, Péstel, Ryléeff,
and Muravióv-Apóstol.

The beauty of the style of Hérzen—of whom
Turguéneff has truly said that he wrote in tears and
blood, and that no other Russian had ever so written—
the breadth of his ideas, and his deep love of Russia
took possession of me, and I used to read and re-read
those pages, even more full of heart than of brain.

In 1859, or early in 1860, I began to edit my first
revolutionary paper. At that age, what could I be but
a constitutionalist?—and my paper advocated the
necessity of a constitution for Russia. I wrote about
the foolish expenses of the Court, the sums of money
which were spent at Nice to keep quite a squadron of
the navy in attendance on the dowager Empress, who
died in 1860; I mentioned the misdeeds of the functionaries which I continually heard spoken of, and I
urged the necessity of constitutional rule. I wrote
three copies of my paper, and slipped them into the
desks of three comrades of the higher forms, who, I
thought, might be interested in public affairs. I asked
my readers to put their remarks behind the Scotch
grandfather clock in our library.

With a throbbing heart, I went next day to see if there was something for me behind the clock. Two notes were there, indeed. Two comrades wrote that they fully sympathized with my paper, and only advised me not to risk too much. I wrote my second number, still more vigorously insisting upon the necessity of uniting all forces in the name of liberty. But this time there was no reply behind the clock. Instead the two comrades came to me.

'We are sure,' they said, 'that it is you who edit the paper, and we want to talk about it. We are quite agreed with you, and we are here to say, "Let us be friends." Your paper has done its work—it has brought us together; but there is no need to continue it. In all the school there are only two more who would take any interest in such matters, while if it becomes known that there is a paper of this kind the consequences will be terrible for all of us. Let us constitute a circle and talk about everything; perhaps we shall put something into the heads of a few others.'

This was so sensible that I could only agree, and we sealed our union by a hearty shaking of hands. From that time we three became firm friends, and used to read a great deal together and discuss all sorts of things.

The abolition of serfdom was the question which then engrossed the attention of all thinking men.

The Revolution of 1848 had had its distinct echo in the hearts of the Russian peasant folk, and from the year 1850 the insurrections of revolted serfs began to take serious proportions. When the Crimean war broke out, and militia was levied all over Russia, these revolts spread with a violence never before heard of. Several serf-owners were killed by their serfs, and the peasant uprisings became so serious that whole regiments, with artillery, were sent to quell them, whereas in former times small detachments of soldiers would have been sufficient to terrorize the peasants into obedience.

These outbreaks on the one side, and the profound aversion to serfdom which had grown up in the generation which came to the front with the advent of Alexander II. to the throne, rendered the emancipation of the peasants more and more imperative. The emperor, himself averse to serfdom, and supported, or rather influenced, in his own family by his wife, his brother Constantine, and the grand duchess Hélène Pávlovna, took the first steps in that direction. His intention was that the initiative of the reform should come from the nobility, the serf-owners themselves. But in no province of Russia could the nobility be induced to send a petition to the Tsar to that effect. In March 1856 he himself addressed the Moscow nobility on the necessity of such a step; but a stubborn silence was all their reply to his speech, so that Alexander II., growing quite angry, concluded with those memorable words of Hérzen: ' It is better, gentlemen, that it should come from above than to wait till it comes from beneath.' Even these words had no effect, and it was to the provinces of Old Poland —Gródno, Wílno, and Kóvno—where Napoleon I. had abolished serfdom (on paper) in 1812, that recourse was had. The Governor-General of those provinces,

Nazímoff, managed to obtain the desired address from the Polish nobility. In November 1857 the famous 'rescript' to the Governor-General of the Lithuanian provinces, announcing the intention of the emperor to abolish serfdom, was launched, and we read, with tears in our eyes, the beautiful article of Hérzen, 'Thou hast conquered, Galilean,' in which the refugees in London declared that they would no more look upon Alexander II. as an enemy, but would support him in the great work of emancipation.

The attitude of the peasants was very remarkable. No sooner had the news spread that the liberation long sighed for was coming than the insurrections nearly stopped. The peasants waited now, and during a journey which Alexander made in Middle Russia they flocked around him as he passed, beseeching him to grant them liberty—a petition, however, which Alexander received with great repugnance. It is most remarkable—so strong is the force of tradition—that the rumour went among the peasants that it was Napoleon III. who had required of the Tsar, in the treaty of peace, that the peasants should be freed. I frequently heard this rumour; and on the very eve of the emancipation they seemed to doubt that it would be done without pressure from abroad. 'Nothing will be done unless Garibaldi comes,' was the reply which a peasant made at St. Petersburg to a comrade of mine who talked to him about 'freedom coming.'

But after these moments of general rejoicing years of incertitude and disquiet followed. Specially appointed committees in the provinces and at St. Petersburg discussed the proposed liberation of the serfs, but the intentions of Alexander II. seemed unsettled. A check was continually put upon the press, in order to prevent it from discussing details. Sinister rumours circulated at St. Petersburg and reached our corps.

There was no lack of young men amongst the nobility who earnestly worked for a frank abolition of the old servitude; but the serfdom party drew closer and closer round the emperor, and got power over his mind. They whispered into his ears that the day serfdom was abolished the peasants would begin to kill the landlords wholesale, and Russia would witness a new Pugachóff uprising, far more terrible than that of 1773. Alexander, who was a man of weak character, only too readily lent his ear to such predictions. But the huge machine for working out the emancipation law had been set to work. The committees had their sittings; scores of schemes of emancipation, addressed to the emperor, circulated in manuscript or were printed in London. Hérzen, seconded by Turguéneff, who kept him well informed about all that was going on in government circles, discussed in his 'Bell' and his 'Polar Star' the details of the various schemes, and Chernyshévsky in the 'Contemporary' (*Sovreménnik*). The Slavophiles, especially Aksákoff and Bélyáeff, had taken advantage of the first moments of relative freedom allowed the press, to give the matter a wide publicity in Russia, and to discuss the features of the emancipation with a thorough understanding of its technical aspects. All intellectual St. Petersburg was with Hérzen, and particularly with Chernyshévsky, and I remember how the officers of the Horse Guards, whom I saw on

Sundays, after the church parade, at the home of my cousin (Dmítri Nikoláevich Kropótkin, who was aide-de-camp of that regiment and aide-de-camp of the emperor), used to side with Chernyshévsky, the leader of the advanced party in the emancipation struggle. The whole disposition of St. Petersburg, in the drawing-rooms and in the street, was such that it was impossible to go back. The liberation of the serfs had to be accomplished; and another important point was won—the liberated serfs would receive, besides their homesteads, the land that they had hitherto cultivated for themselves.

However, the party of the old nobility were not discouraged. They centred their efforts on obtaining a postponement of the reform, on reducing the size of the allotments, and on imposing upon the emancipated serfs so high a redemption tax for the land that it would render their economical freedom illusory; and in this they fully succeeded. Alexander II. dismissed the real soul of the whole business, Nikolái Milútin (brother of the minister of war), saying to him, 'I am so sorry to part with you, but I must: the nobility describe you as one of the Reds.' The first committees, which had worked out the scheme of emancipation, were dismissed, too, and new committees revised the whole work in the interest of the serf-owners; the press was muzzled once more.

Things assumed a very gloomy aspect. The question whether the liberation would take place at all was now asked. I feverishly followed the struggle, and every Sunday, when my comrades returned from their homes, I asked them what their parents said. By the end of 1860 the news became worse and worse. 'The Valúeff party has got the upper hand.' 'They intend to revise the whole work.' 'The relatives of the Princess X. [a friend of the Tsar] work hard upon him.' 'The liberation will be postponed : they fear a revolution.'

In January 1861 slightly better rumours began to circulate, and it was generally hoped that something would be heard of the emancipation on the day of the emperor's accession to the throne, February 19.

The 19th came, but it brought nothing with it. I was on that day at the palace. There was no grand *levée*, only a small one ; and pages of the second form were sent to such *levées* in order to get accustomed to the palace ways. It was my turn that day ; and as I was seeing off one of the grand duchesses who came to the palace to assist at the Mass, her husband did not appear and I went to fetch him. He was called out of the emperor's study, and I told him, in a half jocose way, of the perplexity of his wife, without having the slightest suspicion of the important matters that may have been talked of in the study at that time. Apart from a few of the initiated, no one in the palace suspected that the manifesto had been signed on February 19, and was kept back for a fortnight only because the next Sunday, the 26th, was the beginning of the carnival week, and it was feared that, owing to the drinking which goes on in the villages during the carnival, peasant insurrections might break out. Even the carnival fair, which used to be held at St. Petersburg on the square near the winter palace, was removed that year to another square, from fear of a popular insurrection in the capital. Most sanguinary instructions had been issued to the army as to the ways of repressing peasant uprisings.

A fortnight later, on the last Sunday of the carnival (March 5, or rather March 17, new style), I was at the corps, having to take part in the military parade at the riding-school. I was still in bed, when my soldier servant, Ivánoff, dashed in with the tea tray, exclaiming, 'Prince, freedom! The manifesto is posted on the Gostínoi Dvor' (the shops opposite the corps).

'Did you see it yourself?'

'Yes. People stand round; one reads, the others listen. It *is* freedom!'

In a couple of minutes I was dressed and out. A comrade was coming in.

'Kropótkin, freedom!' he shouted. 'Here is the manifesto. My uncle learned last night that it would be read at the early Mass at the Isaac Cathedral; so we went. There were not many people there; peasants only. The manifesto was read and distributed after the Mass. They well understood what it meant: when I came out of the church, two peasants, who stood in the gateway, said to me in such a droll way, "Well, sir? now—all gone?"' And he mimicked how they had shown him the way out. Years of expectation were in that gesture of sending away the master.

I read and re-read the manifesto. It was written in an elevated style by the old metropolitan of Moscow, Philarète, but with a useless mixture of Russian and old Slavonian which obscured the sense. It was liberty; but it was not liberty yet, the peasants having to remain serfs for two years more, till February 19, 1863. Notwithstanding all this, one thing was evident: serfdom was abolished, and the liberated serfs would get the land and their homesteads. They would have to pay for it, but the old stain of slavery was removed. They would be slaves no more; the reaction had *not* got the upper hand.

We went to the parade; and when all the military performances were over, Alexander II., remaining on horseback, loudly called out, 'The officers to me!' They gathered round him, and he began, in a loud voice, a speech about the great event of the day.

'The officers . . . the representatives of the nobility in the army'—these scraps of sentences reached our ears—'an end has been put to centuries of injustice . . . . I expect sacrifices from the nobility . . . the loyal nobility will gather round the throne' . . . and so on. Enthusiastic hurrahs resounded amongst the officers as he ended.

We ran rather than marched back on our way to the corps—hurrying to be in time for the Italian opera, of which the last performance in the season was to be given that afternoon; some manifestation was sure to take place then. Our military attire was flung off with great haste, and several of us dashed, lightfooted, to the sixth-story gallery. The house was crowded.

During the first entr'acte the smoking room of the opera filled with excited young men, who all talked to one another, whether acquainted or not. We planned at once to return to the hall, and to sing, with the whole public in a mass choir, the hymn 'God Save the Tsar.'

However, sounds of music reached our ears, and we all hurried back to the hall. The band of the opera was already playing the hymn, which was drowned immediately in enthusiastic hurrahs coming from the galleries, the boxes, the pit. I saw Bavéri, the conductor, waving his stick, but not a sound could be heard from the powerful band. Then Bavéri stopped, but the hurrahs continued. I saw the stick waved again in the air ; I saw the fiddle bows moving and musicians blowing the brass instruments, but again the sound of voices overwhelmed the band. Bavéri began conducting the hymn once more, and it was only by the end of that third repetition that isolated sounds of the brass instruments pierced through the clamour of human voices.

The same enthusiasm was in the streets. Crowds of peasants and educated men stood in front of the palace, shouting hurrahs, and the Tsar could not appear without being followed by demonstrative crowds running after his carriage. Hérzen was right when, two years later, as Alexander was drowning the Polish insurrection in blood, and 'Muraviôff the Hanger' was strangling it on the scaffold, he wrote, 'Alexander Nikoláevich, why did you not die on that day ? Your name would have been transmitted in history as that of a hero.'

Where were the uprisings which had been predicted by the champions of slavery? Conditions more indefinite than those which had been created by the

Polozhénie (the emancipation law) could not have been invented. If anything could have provoked revolts, it was precisely the perplexing vagueness of the conditions created by the new law. And yet—except in two places where there were insurrections, and a very few other spots where small disturbances, entirely due to misunderstandings and immediately appeased, took place—Russia remained quiet, more quiet than ever. With their usual good sense, the peasants had understood that serfdom was done away with, that 'freedom had come,' and they accepted the conditions imposed upon them, although these conditions were very heavy.

I was in Nikólskoye in August 1861, and again in the summer of 1862, and I was struck with the quiet intelligent way in which the peasants had accepted the new conditions. They knew perfectly well how difficult it would be to pay the redemption tax for the land, which was in reality an indemnity to the nobles in lieu of the obligations of serfdom. But they so much valued the abolition of their personal enslavement that they accepted the ruinous charges—not without murmuring, but as a hard necessity—the moment that personal freedom was obtained. For the first months they kept two holidays a week, saying that it was a sin to work on Friday; but when the summer came they resumed work with even more energy than before.

When I saw our Nikólskoye peasants, fifteen months after the liberation, I could not but admire them. Their inborn good nature and softness remained with them, but all traces of servility had disappeared. They talked to their masters as equals talk to equals, as if they never had stood in different relations. Besides,

such men came out from among them as could make a
stand for their rights. The Polozhénie was a large and
difficult book, which it took me a good deal of time to
understand; but when Vasíli Ivánoff, the elder of Nikólskoye, came one day to ask me to explain to him some
obscurity in it, I saw that he, who was not even a fluent
reader, had admirably found his way amongst the intricacies of the chapters and paragraphs of the law.

.The 'household people'—that is, the servants—
came out the worst of all. They got no land, and
would hardly have known what to do with it if they
had. They got freedom, and nothing besides. In our
neighbourhood nearly all of them left their masters ;
none, for example, remained in the household of my
father. They went in search of positions elsewhere, and
a number of them found employment at once with the
merchant class, who were proud of having the coachman
of Prince So-and-So, or the cook of General So-and-So.
Those who knew a trade found work in the towns : for
instance, my father's band remained a band, and made
a good living at Kalúga, retaining amiable relations with
us. But those who had no trade had hard times before
them, and yet the majority preferred to live anyhow
rather than remain with their old masters.

As to the landlords, while the larger ones made all
possible efforts at St. Petersburg to re-introduce the old
conditions under one name or another (they succeeded
in doing so to some extent under Alexander III.), by far
the greater number submitted to the abolition of serfdom
as to a sort of necessary calamity. The young generation gave to Russia that remarkable staff of ' peace
mediators ' and justices of the peace who contributed so

much to the peaceful issue of the emancipation. As to
the old generation, most of them had already discounted
the considerable sums of money they were to receive
from the peasants for the land which was granted to the
liberated serfs, and which was valued much above its
market price ; they schemed as to how they would
squander that money in the restaurants of the capitals,
or at the green tables in gambling. And they did
squander it, almost all of them, as soon as they got it.

For many landlords the liberation of the serfs was
an excellent money transaction. Thus, land which my
father, in anticipation of the emancipation, sold in
parcels at the rate of eleven roubles the Russian acre,
was now estimated at forty roubles in the peasants'
allotments—that is, three and a half times above its
market value—and this was the rule in all our neighbourhood ; while in my father's Tambóv estate, on the
prairies, the *mir*—that is, the village community—
rented all his land for twelve years at a price which
represented twice as much as he used to get from that
land by cultivating it with servile labour.

Eleven years after that memorable time I went to
the Tambóv estate, which I had inherited from my
father. I stayed there for a few weeks, and on the
evening of my departure our village priest—an intelligent man of independent opinions, such as one meets
occasionally in our southern provinces—went out for a
walk round the village. The sunset was glorious ; a
balmy air came from the prairies. He found a middle-
aged peasant—Antón Savélieff—sitting on a small
eminence outside the village and reading a book of

psalms. The peasant hardly knew how to spell in Old Slavonic, and often he would read a book from the last page, turning the pages backward; it was the process of reading which he liked most, and then a word would strike him, and its repetition pleased him. He was reading now a psalm of which each verse began with the word ' rejoice.'

' What are you reading?' he was asked.

' Well, father, I will tell you,' was his reply. ' Fourteen years ago the old prince came here. It was in the winter. I had just returned home, quite frozen. A snowstorm was raging. I had scarcely begun undressing when we heard a knock at the window : it was the elder, who was shouting, " Go to the prince! He wants you!" We all—my wife and our children—were thunderstricken. " What can he want of you?" my wife cried in alarm. I signed myself with the cross and went; the snowstorm almost blinded me as I crossed the bridge. Well, it ended all right. The old prince was taking his afternoon sleep, and when he woke up he asked me if I knew plastering work, and only told me, " Come to-morrow to repair the plaster in that room." So I went home quite happy, and when I came to the bridge I found my wife standing there. She had stood there all the time in the snowstorm, with the baby in her arms, waiting for me. " What has happened, Savélich?" she cried. " Well," I said, "no harm ; he only asked me to make some repairs." That, father, was under the old prince. And now, the young prince came here the other day. I went to see him, and found him in the garden, at the tea table, in the shadow of the house; you, father, sat with him, and the elder of the canton, with his mayor's chain upon his breast. " Will you have tea, Savélich ? " he asks me. " Take a chair. Petr Grigórieff "—he says that to the old one—" give us one more chair." And Petr Grigórieff—you know what a terror for us he was when he was the manager of the old prince—brought the chair, and we all sat round the tea table, talking, and he poured out tea for all of us. Well, now, father, the evening is so beautiful, the balm comes from the prairies, and I sit and read, " Rejoice ! Rejoice ! " '·

This is what the abolition of serfdom meant for the peasants.

IX

In June 1861 I was nominated sergeant of the Corps of Pages. Some of our officers, I must say, did not like the idea of it, saying that there would be no discipline with me acting as a sergeant, but it could not be helped ; it was usually the first pupil of the upper form who was nominated sergeant, and I had been at the top of our form for several years in succession. This appointment was considered very enviable, not only because the sergeant occupied a privileged position in the school and was treated like an officer, but especially because he was also the page de chambre of the emperor for the time being ; and to be personally known to the emperor was of course considered as a stepping-stone to further distinctions. The most important point to me was, however, that it freed me from all the drudgery of the inner service of the school, which fell on the pages de chambre, and that I should have for my studies a separate room where I could isolate myself from the bustle of the school. True, there was also an important drawback to it : I had always found it tedious to pace up and down, many times a day, the whole length of our rooms, and used therefore to run the distance full speed, which was severely prohibited ; and now I should have to walk very solemnly, with the service book under my arm, instead of running ! A consultation was even held among a few friends of mine upon this serious matter, and it was decided that from time to time I could still find opportunities to take my favourite runs ; as to my relations with all the others, it depended upon myself to put them on a new comrade-like footing, and this I did.

The pages de chambre had to be at the palace frequently, in attendance at the great and small *levées*, the balls, the receptions, the gala dinners, and so on. During Christmas, New Year, and Easter weeks we were summoned to the palace almost every day, and sometimes twice a day. Moreover, in my military capacity of sergeant I had to report to the emperor every Sunday, at the parade in the riding-school, that ' all was well at the company of the Corps of Pages,' even when one-third of the school was ill of some contagious disease. ' Shall I not report to-day that all is not quite well ? ' I asked the colonel on this occasion. ' God bless you,' was his reply, ' you ought only to say so if there were an insurrection ! '

Court life has undoubtedly much that is picturesque

about it. With its elegant refinement of manners—superficial though it may be—its strict etiquette, and its brilliant surroundings, it is certainly meant to be impressive. A great *levée* is a fine pageant, and even the simple reception of a few ladies by the empress becomes quite different from a common call when it takes place in a richly decorated drawing-room of the palace — the guests ushered by chamberlains in gold-embroidered uniforms, the hostess followed by brilliantly dressed pages and a suite of ladies, and everything conducted with striking solemnity. To be an actor in the Court ceremonies, in attendance upon the chief personages, offered something more than the mere interest of curiosity for a boy of my age. Besides, I then looked upon Alexander II. as a sort of hero; a man who attached no importance to the Court ceremonies, but who, at this period of his reign, began his working day at six in the morning, and was engaged in a hard struggle with a powerful reactionary party in order to carry through a series of reforms in which the abolition of serfdom was only the first step.

But gradually, as I saw more of the spectacular side of Court life, and caught now and then a glimpse of what was going on behind the scenes, I realized, not only the futility of these shows and the things they were intended to conceal, but also that these small things so much absorbed the Court as to prevent consideration of matters of far greater importance. The realities were often lost in the acting. And then from Alexander II. himself slowly faded the aureole with which my imagination had surrounded him; so that by the end of the year, even if at the outset I had cherished some illusions as to useful activity in the spheres nearest to the palace, I should have retained none.

On every important holiday, as also on the birth-days and name days of the emperor and empress, on the coronation day, and on other similar occasions, a great *levée* was held at the palace. Thousands of generals and officers of all ranks, down to that of captain, as well as the high functionaries of the civil service, were arranged in lines in the immense halls of the palace, to bow at the passage of the emperor and his family, as they solemnly proceeded to the church. All the members of the imperial family came on those days to the palace, meeting together in a drawing-room and merrily chatting till the moment arrived for putting on the mask of solemnity. Then the column was formed. The emperor, giving his hand to the empress, opened the march. He was followed by his page de chambre, and he in turn by the general aide-de-camp, the aide-de-camp on duty that day, and the minister of the imperial household ; while the empress, or rather the immense train of her dress, was attended by her two pages de chambre, who had to support the train at the turnings and to spread it out again in all its beauty. The heir-apparent, who was a young man of eighteen, and all the other grand dukes and duchesses, came next, in the order of their right of succession to the throne—each of the grand duchesses followed by her page de chambre ; then there was a long procession of the ladies in atten-dance, old and young, all wearing the so-called Russian costume—that is, an evening dress which was supposed to resemble the costume worn by the women of Old Russia.

As the procession passed I could see how each of the eldest military and civil functionaries, before making his bow, would try to catch the eye of the emperor, and if he had his bow acknowledged by a smiling look of the Tsar, or by a hardly perceptible nod of the head, or perchance by a word or two, he would look round upon his neighbours, full of pride, in the expectation of their congratulations.

From the church the procession returned in the same way, and then everyone hurried back to his own affairs. Apart from a few devotees and some young ladies, not one in ten present at these *levées* regarded them otherwise than as a tedious duty.

Twice or thrice during the winter great balls were given at the palace, and thousands of people were invited to them. After the emperor had opened the dances with a polonaise, full liberty was left to every one to enjoy the time as he liked. There was plenty of room in the immense brightly illuminated halls, where young girls were easily lost to the watchful eyes of their parents and aunts, and many thoroughly enjoyed the dances and the supper, during which the young people managed to be left to themselves.

My duties at these balls were rather difficult. Alexander II. did not dance, nor did he sit down, but he moved all the time amongst his guests, his page de chambre having to follow him at a distance, so as to be within easy call, and yet not inconveniently near. This combination of presence with absence was not easy to attain, nor did the emperor require it: he would have preferred to be left entirely to himself; but such was the tradition, and he had to submit to it. The worst was when he entered a dense crowd of ladies who stood round the circle in which the grand dukes danced, and slowly circulated among them. It was not at all easy to make a way through this living garden, which opened to give passage to the emperor, but closed in immediately behind him. Instead of dancing themselves, hundreds of ladies and girls stood there, closely packed, each in the expectation that one of the grand dukes would perhaps notice her and invite her to dance a waltz or a polka. Such was the influence of the Court upon St. Petersburg society that if one of the grand dukes cast his eye upon a girl, her parents would do all in their power to make their child fall madly in love with the great personage, even though they knew well that no marriage could result from it — the Russian grand dukes not being allowed to marry 'subjects' of the Tsar. The conversations which I once heard in a 'respectable' family, connected with the Court, after the heir-apparent had danced twice·or thrice with a girl of seventeen, and the hopes which were expressed by her parents, surpassed all that I could possibly have imagined.

Every time that we were at the palace we had lunch or dinner there, and the footmen would whisper to us bits of news from the scandalous chronicle of the place, whether we cared for it or not. They knew everything that was going on in the different palaces — that was their domain. For truth's sake, I must say that during the year which I speak of that sort of chronicle was not as rich in events as it became in the seventies. The brothers of the Tsar were only recently married, and his sons were all very young. But the relations of the emperor himself with the Princess X., whom Turguéneff has so admirably depicted in 'Smoke' under the name of Irène, were even more freely spoken of by the servants than by St. Petersburg society. One day, however, when we entered the room where we used to dress, we were told, 'The X. has to-day got her dismissal — a complete one this time.' Half an hour later we saw the lady in question coming to assist at Mass, with her eyes swollen from weeping, and swallowing her tears during the Mass, while the other ladies managed so to stand at a distance from her as to put her in evidence. The footmen were already informed about the incident, and commented upon it in their own way. There was something truly repulsive in the talk of these men, who the day before would have crouched down before the same lady.

The system of espionage which is exercised in the palace, especially around the emperor himself, would seem almost incredible to the uninitiated. The following incident will give some idea of it. A few years later, one of the grand dukes received a severe lesson from a St. Petersburg gentleman. The latter had forbidden the grand duke his house, but, returning home unexpectedly, he found him in his drawing-room and rushed upon him with his lifted stick. The young man dashed down the staircase, and was already jumping into his carriage when the pursuer caught him, and dealt him a blow with his stick. The policeman who stood at the door saw the adventure and ran to report it to the chief of the police, General Trépoff, who, in his turn, jumped into his carriage and hastened to the emperor, to be the first to report the 'sad incident.' Alexander II. summoned the grand duke and had a talk with him. A couple of days later, an old functionary who belonged to the Third Section of the emperor's chancery — that is, to the state police — and who was a friend at the house of one of my comrades, related the whole conversation. 'The emperor,' he informed us, 'was very angry, and said to the grand duke in conclusion, " You should know better how to manage your little affairs." ' He was asked, of course, how he could know anything about a private conversation, but the reply was very characteristic : ' The words and the opinions of his Majesty must be known to our department. How otherwise could such a delicate institution as the state police be managed ? Be sure that the emperor is the most closely watched person in all St. Petersburg.'

There was no boasting in these words. Every minister, every governor-general, before entering the emperor's study with his reports, had a talk with the private valet of the emperor, to know what was the mood of the master that day ; and according to that mood he either laid before him some knotty affair, or let it lie at the bottom of his portfolio in hope of a more lucky day. The governor-general of East Siberia, when he came to St. Petersburg, always sent his private aide-de-camp with a handsome gift to the private valet of the emperor. ' There are days,' he used to say, ' when the emperor would get into a rage, and order a searching inquest upon everyone and myself, if I should lay before him on such a day certain reports ; whereas there are other days when all will go off quite

smoothly. A precious man that valet is.' To know
from day to day the frame of mind of the emperor was
a substantial part of the art of retaining a high position
—an art which later on Count Shuváloff and General
Trépoff understood to perfection ; also Count Ignátieff,
who, I suppose from what I saw of him, possessed that
art even without the help of the valet.

At the beginning of my service I felt a great
admiration for Alexander II., the liberator of the serfs.
Imagination often carries a boy beyond the realities of
the moment, and my frame of mind at that time was
such that if an attempt had been made in my presence
upon the Tsar I should have covered him with my
body. One day, at the beginning of January 1862, I
saw him leave the procession and rapidly walk alone
toward the halls where parts of all the regiments of
the St. Petersburg garrison were aligned for a parade.
This parade usually took place outdoors, but this year,
on account of the frost, it was held indoors, and
Alexander II., who generally galloped at full speed in
front of the troops at the reviews, had now to march
in front of the regiments. I knew that my Court duties
ended as soon as the emperor appeared in his capacity of military commander of the troops, and that
I had to follow him to this spot, but no further.
However, on looking round, I saw that he was quite
alone. The two aides-de-camp had disappeared, and
there was with him not a single man of his suite. ' I
will not leave him alone ! ' I said to myself, and
followed him.

Whether Alexander II. was in a great hurry that

day, or had other reasons to wish that the review should be over as soon as possible, I cannot say, but he dashed in front of the troops, and marched along their rows at such a speed, making such big and rapid steps—he was very tall—that I had the greatest difficulty in following him at my most rapid pace, and in places had almost to run in order to keep close behind him. He hurried as if he ran away from a danger. His excitement communicated itself to me, and every moment I was ready to jump in front of him, regretting only that I had on my ordnance sword and not my own sword, with a Toledo blade, which pierced coppers and was a far better weapon. It was only after he had passed in front of the last battalion that he slackened his pace, and, on entering another hall, looked round, to meet my eyes glittering with the excitement of that mad march. The younger aide-de-camp was running at full speed, two halls behind. I was prepared to get a severe scolding, instead of which Alexander II. said to me, perhaps betraying his own inner thoughts : ' You here ? Brave boy ! ' and as he slowly walked away he turned into space that problematic, absent-minded gaze which I had begun often to notice.

Such was then the attitude of my mind. However, various small incidents, as well as the reactionary character which the policy of Alexander II. was decidedly taking, instilled more and more doubts into my heart. Every year, on January 6, a half Christian and half pagan ceremony of sanctifying the waters is performed in Russia. It is also performed at the palace. A pavilion is built on the Nevá River, opposite the palace, and the imperial family, headed by the clergy, proceed from the palace, across the superb quay, to the pavilion, where a Te Deum is sung and the cross is plunged into the water of the river. Thousands of people stand on the quay and on the ice of the Nevá to witness the ceremony from a distance. All have to stand bareheaded during the service. This year, as the frost was rather sharp, an old general had put on a wig, and in the hurry of drawing on his cape, his wig had been dislodged and now lay across his head, without his noticing it. The grand duke Constantine, having caught sight of it, laughed the whole time the Te Deum was being sung, with the younger grand dukes, looking in the direction of the unhappy general, who smiled stupidly without knowing why he was the cause of so much hilarity. Constantine finally whispered to the emperor, who also looked at the general and laughed.

A few minutes later, as the procession once more crossed the quay, on its way back to the palace, an old peasant, bareheaded too, pushed himself through the double hedge of soldiers who lined the path of the procession, and fell on his knees just at the feet of the emperor, holding out a petition, and crying with tears in his eyes, 'Father, defend us!' Ages of oppression of the Russian peasantry was in this exclamation; but Alexander II., who a few minutes before laughed during the church service at a wig lying the wrong way, now passed by the peasant without taking the slightest notice of him. I was close behind him, and only saw in him a shudder of fear at the sudden appearance of the peasant, after which he went on without deigning even to cast a glance on the human figure at his feet. I looked round. The aides-de-camp were not there ; the grand duke Constantine, who followed, took no more notice of the peasant than his brother did ; there was nobody even to take the petition, so that I took it, although I knew that I should get a scolding for doing so. It was not my business to receive petitions, but I remembered what it must have cost the peasant before he could make his way to the capital, and then through the lines of police and soldiers who surrounded the procession. Like all peasants who hand petitions to the Tsar, he was going to be put under arrest, for no one knows how long.

On the day of the emancipation of the serfs Alexander II. was worshipped at St. Petersburg ; but it is most remarkable that, apart from that moment of general enthusiasm, he had not the love of the city. His brother Nicholas—no one could say why—was at least very popular among the small trades-people and the cabmen ; but neither Alexander II., nor his brother Constantine, the leader of the reform party, nor his third brother, Michael, had won the hearts of any class of people in St. Petersburg. Alexander II. had retained too much of the despotic character of his father, which pierced now and then through his usually good-natured manners. He easily lost his temper, and often treated his courtiers in the most contemptuous way. He was not what one would describe as a reliable man, either in his policy or in his personal sympathies, and he was vindictive. I doubt whether he was sincerely attached to anyone. Some of the

men in his nearest surroundings were of the worst
description—Count Adlerberg, for instance, who made
him pay over and over again his enormous debts, and
others renowned for their colossal thefts. From the
beginning of 1862 he commenced to show himself
capable of reviving the worst practices of his father's
reign. It was known that he still wanted to carry
through a series of important reforms in the judicial
organization and in the army; that the terrible corporal
punishments were about to be abolished, and that a
sort of local self-government, and perhaps a constitution of some sort, would be granted. But the slightest
disturbance was repressed under his orders with a
stern severity ; he took each movement as a personal
offence, so that at any moment one might expect from
him the most reactionary measures.

The disorders which broke out at the universities of
St. Petersburg, Moscow, and Kazán in October 1861
were repressed with an ever-increasing strictness. The
university of St. Petersburg was closed, and although free
courses were opened by most of the professors at the
Town Hall, they also were soon closed, and the best
professors left the university. Immediately after the
abolition of serfdom, a great movement began for the
opening of Sunday schools ; they were opened everywhere by private persons and corporations—all the
teachers being volunteers—and the peasants and
workers, old and young, flocked to these schools.
Officers, students, even a few pages, became teachers ;
and such excellent methods were worked out that
(Russian having a phonetic spelling) we succeeded in
teaching a peasant to read in nine or ten lessons. But

suddenly all Sunday schools, in which the mass of the peasantry would have learned to read in a few years, without any expenditure by the State, were closed.   In Poland, where a series of patriotic manifestations had begun, the Cossacks were sent out to disperse the crowds with their whips, and to arrest hundreds of people in the churches with their usual brutality.   Men were shot in the streets of Warsaw by the end of 1861, and for the suppression of the few peasant insurrec·tions which broke out the horrible flogging through the double line of soldiers—that favourite punishment of Nicholas I.—was applied.   The despot that Alexander II. became in the years 1870–81 was foreshadowed in 1862.

Of all the imperial family, undoubtedly the most sympathetic was the empress Marie Alexándrovna. She was sincere, and when she said something pleasant she meant it.   The way in which she once thanked me for a little courtesy (it was after her reception of the ambassador of the United States, who had just come to St. Petersburg) deeply impressed me : it was not the way of a lady spoiled by courtesies, as an empress is supposed to be.   She certainly was not happy in her home life ; nor was she liked by the ladies of the court, who found her too severe, and could not understand why she should take so much to heart the *étourderies* of her husband.   It is now known that she played a by no means unimportant part in bringing about the abolition of serfdom.   But at that time her influence in this direction seems to have been little known, the grand duke Constantine and the grand duchess Hélène

Pávlovna, who was the main support of Nicholas Milútin at the Court, being considered the two leaders of the reform party in the palace spheres.   The empress was better known for the decisive part she had taken in the creation of girls' gymnasia (high schools), which received from the outset a high standard of organization and a truly democratic character.   Her friendly relations with Ushínsky, a great pedagogist, saved him from sharing the fate of all men of mark of that time— that is, exile.

Being very well educated herself, Marie Alexándrovna did her best to give a good education to her eldest son.   The best men in all branches of knowledge were sought as teachers, and she even invited for that purpose Kavélin, although she knew well his friendly relations with Hérzen.   When he mentioned to her that friendship, she replied that she had no grudge against Hérzen, except for his violent language about the empress dowager.

The heir-apparent was extremely handsome—perhaps, even too femininely handsome.   He was not proud in the least, and during the *levées* he used to chatter in the most comradelike way with the pages de chambre.   (I even remember, at the reception of the diplomatic corps on New Year's Day, trying to make him appreciate the simplicity of the uniform of the ambassador of the United States as compared with the parrot-coloured uniforms of the other ambassadors.)   However, those who knew him well described him as profoundly egoistic, a man absolutely incapable of contracting an attachment to anyone.   This feature was prominent in him, even more than it was in his father.

As to his education, all the pains taken by his mother were of no avail. In August 1861 his examinations, which were made in the presence of his father, proved to be a dead failure, and I remember Alexander II., at a parade of which the heir-apparent was the commander, and during which he made some mistake, loudly shouting out, so that everyone would hear it, ' Even that you could not learn ! ' He died, as is known, at the age of twenty-two, from some disease of the spinal cord.

His brother, Alexander, who became the heir-apparent in 1865, and later on was Alexander III., was a decided contrast to Nikolái Alexándrovich. He reminded me so much of Paul I. by his face, his figure, and his contemplation of his own grandeur, that I used to say, ' If he ever reigns, he will be another Paul I. in the Gátchina palace, and will have the same end as his great-grandfather had at the hands of his own courtiers.' He obstinately refused to learn. It was rumoured that Alexander II., having had so many difficulties with his brother Constantine, who was better educated than himself, adopted the policy of concentrating all his attention on the heir-apparent and neglecting the education of his other sons ; however, I doubt if such was the case : Alexander Alexándrovich must have been averse to any education from childhood ; in fact, his spelling, which I saw in the telegrams he addressed to his bride at Copenhagen, was unimaginably bad. I cannot render here his Russian spelling, but in French he wrote, *'Ecri* à oncle à propos parade . . . les nouvelles sont *mauvaisent*,' and so on.

He is said to have improved in his manners toward

the end of his life, but in 1870, and also much later, he was a true descendant of Paul I.   I knew at St. Petersburg an officer, of Swedish origin (from Finland), who had been sent to the United States to order rifles for the Russian army.   On his return he had to report about his mission to Alexander Alexándrovich, who had been appointed to superintend the re-arming of the army.   During this interview, the Tsarevich, giving full vent to his violent temper, began to scold the officer, who probably replied with dignity, whereupon the prince fell into a real fit of rage, insulting the officer in bad language.   The officer, who belonged to that type of very loyal but self-respecting men who are frequently met with amongst the Swedish nobility in Russia, left at once, and wrote a letter in which he asked the heir-apparent to apologize within twenty-four hours, adding that if the apology did not come he would shoot himself.   It was a sort of Japanese duel. Alexander Alexándrovich sent no excuses, and the officer kept his word.   I saw him at the house of a warm friend of mine, his intimate friend, when he was expecting every minute to receive the apology.   Next morning he was dead.   The Tsar was very angry with his son, and ordered him to follow the hearse of the officer to the grave.   But even this terrible lesson did not cure the young man of his Románoff haughtiness and impetuosity.

Part Third

SIBERIA

I

In the middle of May 1862, a few weeks before our promotion, I was told one day by the Captain to make up the final list of the regiments which each of us intended to join. We had the choice of all the regiments of the Guards, which we could enter with the first officer's grade, and of the Army with the third grade of lieutenant. I took a list of our form, and went the round of my comrades. Everyone knew well the regiment he was going to join, most of them already wearing in the garden the officer's cap of that regiment.

'Her Majesty's Cuirassiers,' 'The Body Guard Preobrazhénsky,' 'The Horse Guards,' were the replies which I inscribed in my list.

'But you, Kropótkin? The artillery? The Cossacks?' I was asked on all sides. I could not stand these questions, and at last, asking a comrade to complete the list, I went to my room to think once more over my final decision.

That I should not enter a regiment of the Guard, and give my life to parades and court balls, I had settled long before. My dream was to enter the university —to study, to live the student's life. That meant, of course, to break entirely with my father, whose ambitions were quite different, and to rely for my living upon what I might earn by means of lessons. Thousands of Russian students live in that way, and such a life did not frighten me in the least. But—how should I get over the first steps in that life? In a few weeks I should have to leave the school, to don my own clothes, to have my own lodging, and I saw no possibility of providing even the little money which would be required for the most modest start. Then, failing the university, I had been often thinking of late that I could enter the Artillery Academy. That would free me for two years from the drudgery of military service, and by the side of the military sciences I could study mathematics and physics. But the wind of reaction was blowing, and the officers of the academies had been treated during the previous winter as if they were schoolboys; in two academies they had revolted, and in one of them they had left in a body.

My thoughts turned more and more toward Siberia. The Amúr region had recently been annexed by Russia; I had read all about that Mississippi of the East, the mountains it pierces, the sub-tropical vegetation of its tributary, the Usurí, and my thoughts went further—to the tropical regions which Humboldt had described, and to the great generalizations of Ritter, which I delighted to read. Besides, I reasoned, there is in Siberia an immense field for the application of the great reforms which have been made or are coming: the workers must be few there, and I shall find a field of action to my tastes. The worst would be that I should have to separate from my brother Alexander; but he had been compelled to leave the university of Moscow after the last disorders, and in a year or two, I guessed (and guessed rightly), in one way or another we should be together. There remained only the choice of the regiment in the Amúr region. The Usurí attracted me most; but, alas, there was on the Usurí only one regiment of infantry Cossacks. A Cossack not on horseback—that was too bad for the boy that I still was, and I settled upon 'the mounted Cossacks of the Amúr.'

This I wrote on the list, to the great consternation of all my comrades. 'It is so far,' they said, while my friend Daúroff, seizing the Officers' Handbook, read out of it, to the horror of all present : 'Uniform, black, with a plain red collar without braids; fur bonnet made of dog's fur or any other fur; trousers, gray.'

'Only look at that uniform !' he exclaimed. 'Bother the cap !—you can wear one of wolf or bear fur; but think only of the trousers! Gray, like a soldier of the Train !' The consternation reached its climax after that reading.

I joked as best I could, and took the list to the captain.

'Kropótkin must always have his joke !' he cried. 'Did I not tell you that the list must be sent to the grand duke to-day ?'

I had some difficulty in making him believe that the list really stated my intention.

However, next day my resolution almost gave way when I saw how Klasóvsky took my decision. He had hoped to see me in the university, and had given me lessons in Latin and Greek for that purpose; and I did not dare to tell him what really prevented me from entering the university : I knew that if I told him the

truth he would offer to share with me the little that
he had.

Then my father telegraphed to the director that he
forbade my going to Siberia, and the matter was reported to the grand duke, who was the chief of the
military schools. I was called before his assistant, and
talked about the vegetation of the Amúr and like things,
because I had strong reasons for believing that if I said
I wanted to go to the university and could not afford it,
a bursary would be offered to me by some one of the
imperial family—an offer which by all means I wished
to avoid.

It is impossible to say how all this would have
ended, but an event of much importance—the great fire
at St. Petersburg—brought about in an indirect way a
solution to my difficulties.

On the Monday after Trinity—the day of the
Holy Ghost, which was that year on May 26, o.s.—a
terrible fire broke out in the so-called Apráxin Dvor.
The Apráxin Dvor was an immense space, nearly
half a mile square, which was entirely covered with
small shops—mere shanties of wood—where all sorts
of second- and third-hand goods were sold. Old furniture and bedding, second-hand dresses and books, poured
in from every quarter of the city, and were stored in the
small shanties, in the passages between them, and even
on their roofs. This accumulation of inflammable
materials had at its back the Ministry of the Interior
and its archives, where all the documents concerning
the liberation of the serfs were kept; and in the front
of it, which was lined by a row of shops built of stone,

was the State Bank.   A narrow lane, also bordered with
stone shops, separated the Apráxin Dvor from a wing
of the Corps of Pages, which was occupied by grocery
and oil shops in its lower story and with the apart-
ments of the officers in its upper story.   Almost opposite the Ministry of the Interior, on the other side of a
canal, there were extensive timber yards.   This labyrinth of small shanties and the timber yards opposite
took fire almost at the same moment, at four o'clock in
the afternoon.

If there had been wind on that day, half the city
would have perished in the flames, including the Bank,
several Ministries, the Gostínoi Dvor (another great
block of shops on the Nevsky Perspective), the Corps of
Pages, and the National Library.

I was that afternoon at the Corps, dining at the
house of one of our officers, and we dashed to the spot
as soon as we noticed from the windows the first clouds
of smoke rising in our close neighbourhood.   The sight
was terrific. Like an immense snake, rattling and
whistling, the fire threw itself in all directions, right
and left, enveloped the shanties, and suddenly rose in a
huge column, darting out its whistling tongues to lick
up more shanties with their contents.   Whirlwinds of
smoke and fire were formed; and when the whirls of
burning feathers from the bedding shops began to
sweep about the space, it became impossible to remain
any longer inside the burning market.   The whole had
to be abandoned.

The authorities had entirely lost their heads.   There
was not, at that time, a single steam fire-engine in St.

Petersburg, and it was workmen who suggested bringing one from the iron works of Kólpino, situated twenty
miles by rail from the capital.   When the engine reached
the railway station, it was the people who dragged
it to the conflagration.   Of its four lines of hose, one
was damaged by an unknown hand, and the other three
were directed upon the Ministry of the Interior.

The grand dukes came to the spot and went away
again.   Late in the evening, when the Bank was out
of danger, the emperor also made his appearance, and
said, what everyone knew already, that the Corps of
Pages was now the key of the battle, and must be saved
by all means.   It was evident that if the Corps had
taken fire, the National Library and half of the Nevsky
Perspective would have perished in the flames.

It was the crowd, the people, who did everything to
prevent the fire from spreading further and further.
There was a moment when the Bank was seriously
menaced.   The goods cleared from the shops opposite
were thrown into the Sadóvaya street, and lay in great
heaps upon the walls of the left wing of the Bank.
The articles which covered the street itself continually
took fire, but the people, roasting there in an almost
unbearable heat, prevented the flames from being
communicated to the piles of goods on the other side.
They swore at all the authorities, seeing that there was
not a pump on the spot.   'What are they all doing at
the Ministry of the Interior, when the Bank and the
Foundlings' House are going to take fire ?   They have
all lost their heads !   Where is the chief of police that
he cannot send a fire brigade to the Bank ? ' they said.
I knew the chief, General Annenkoff, personally, as I

had met him once or twice at our sub-inspector's house, whereto he came with his brother the well-known literary critic, and I volunteered to find him. I found him, indeed, walking aimlessly in a street; and when I reported to him the state of affairs, incredible though it may seem, it was to me, a boy, that he gave the order to move one of the fire brigades from the Ministry to the Bank. I exclaimed, of course, that the men would never listen to me, and I asked for a written order; but General Annenkoff had not, or pretended not to have, a scrap of paper, so that I asked one of our officers, L. L. Gosse, to come with me to transmit the order. We at last prevailed upon the captain of one fire brigade—who swore at all the world and at his chiefs— to move his men and engines to the Bank.

The Ministry itself was not on fire; it was the archives which were burning, and many boys, chiefly cadets and pages, together with a number of clerks, carried bundles of papers out of the burning building and loaded them into cabs. Often a bundle would fall out, and the wind, taking possession of its leaves, would strew them about the square. Through the smoke a sinister fire could be seen raging in the timber yards on the other side of the canal.

The narrow lane which separated the Corps of Pages from the Apráxin Dvor was in a deplorable state. The shops which lined it were full of brimstone, oil, turpentine, and the like, and immense tongues of fire of many hues, thrown out by explosions, licked the roofs of the wing of the Corps, which bordered the lane on its other side. The windows and the pilasters under the roof began already to smoulder, while the

pages and some cadets, after having cleared the lodgings,
pumped water through a small fire engine, which
received at long intervals scanty supplies from old-
fashioned barrels, which had to be filled with ladles. A
couple of firemen who stood on the hot roof continually
shouted out, ' Water ! Water ! ' in tones which were
heartrending. I could not stand these cries, and
rushed into the Sadóvaya street, where, by sheer
force, I compelled the driver of one of the barrels
belonging to a police fire brigade to enter our yard
and to supply our pump with water. But when I
attempted to do the same once more, I met with an
absolute refusal from the driver. ' I shall be court-
martialled,' he said, ' if I obey you.' On all sides my
comrades urged me, ' Go and find somebody—the chief
of the police, the grand duke, anyone—and tell them
that without water we shall have to abandon the Corps
to the fire.' ' Ought we not to report to our director ? '
somebody would remark. ' Bother the whole lot ! you
won't find them with a lantern. Go and do it yourself.'

I went once more in search of General Annenkoff,
and was at last told that he must be in the yard of the
Bank. Several officers stood there, indeed, around a
general in whom I recognized the Governor-General of
St. Petersburg, Prince Suvóroff. The gate, however, was
locked, and a Bank official who stood at it refused to
let me in. I insisted, menaced, and finally was admitted.
Then I went straight up to Prince Suvóroff, who was
writing a note on the shoulder of his aide-de-camp.
When I reported to him the state of affairs, his first
question was, ' Who has sent you ? ' ' Nobody—the
comrades,' was my reply. ' So you say the Corps will

soon be on fire?' 'Yes.' He started at once, and seizing in the street an empty hatbox, covered his head with it, in order to protect himself from the scorching heat that came from the burning shops of the Apráxin Dvor and ran full speed to the lane. Empty barrels, straw, wooden boxes, and the like covered the lane, between the flames of the oil shops on the one side and the buildings of our Corps, of which the window frames and the pilasters were smouldering, on the other side. Prince Suvóroff acted resolutely. 'There is a company of soldiers in your garden,' he said to me : 'take a detachment and clear that lane—at once. A hose from the steam engine will be brought here immediately. Keep it playing. I trust it to you personally.'

It was not easy to move the soldiers out of our garden. They had cleared the barrels and boxes of their contents, and with their pockets full of coffee, and with conical lumps of sugar concealed in their *képis*, they were enjoying the warm night under the trees, cracking nuts. No one cared to move till an officer interfered. The lane was cleared, and the pump kept going. The comrades were delighted, and every twenty minutes we relieved the men who directed the jet of water, standing by their side in an almost unbearable heat.

About three or four in the morning it was evident that bounds had been put to the fire ; the danger of its spreading to the Corps was over, and after having quenched my thirst with half a dozen glasses of tea, in a small 'white inn' which happened to be open, I fell, half dead from fatigue, on the first bed that I found unoccupied in the hospital of the corps.

Next morning I woke up early and went to see the

site of the conflagration, when on my return to the corps
I met the Grand Duke Michael, whom I accompanied,
as was my duty, on his round.   The pages, with their
faces quite black from the smoke, with swollen eyes
and inflamed lids, some of them with their hair
burned, raised their heads from the pillows.   It was
hard to recognise them.   They were proud, though,
of feeling that they had not been merely ' white hands,'
and had worked as hard as anyone else.

This visit of the grand duke settled my difficulties.
He asked me why did I conceive that fancy of going to
the Amúr—whether I had friends there ? whether the
Governor-General knew me ? and, learning that I had
no relatives in Siberia and knew nobody there, he
exclaimed, ' But how are you going, then ?   They may
send you to a lonely Cossack village.   What will you
be doing there ?   I had better write about you to the
Governor-General, to recommend you.'

After such an offer I was sure that my father's
objection would be removed ; and so it was.   I was
free to go to Siberia.

This great conflagration became a turning-point
not only in the policy of Alexander II., but also in the
history of Russia in that part of the century.   That it
was not a mere accident was self-evident.   Trinity and
the day of the Holy Ghost are great holidays in Russia
and there was nobody inside the market except a few
watchmen ; besides, the Apráxin market and the timber
yards took fire at the same time, and the conflagration
at St. Petersburg was followed by similar disasters in
several provincial towns.   The fire was lit by some-

body, but by whom? This question remains un-
answered to the present time.

Katkóff, the ex-Whig, who was inspired with personal hatred of Hérzen, and especially of Bakúnin, with
whom he had once to fight a duel, on the very day after
the fire accused the Poles and the Russian revolutionists
of being the cause of it; and that opinion prevailed at
St. Petersburg and Moscow.

Poland was preparing then for the revolution which
broke out in the following January, and the secret
revolutionary government had concluded an alliance
with the London refugees, and had its men in the very
heart of the St. Petersburg administration. Only a
short time after the conflagration occurred, the Lord
Lieutenant of Poland, Count Lüders, was shot at by a
Russian officer; and when the grand duke Constantine
was nominated in his place (with intention, it was said,
of making Poland a separate kingdom for Constantine)
he also was immediately shot at, on June 26. Similar
attempts were made in August against the Marquis
Wielepólsky, the Polish leader of the pro-Russian Union
party. Napoleon III. maintained among the Poles
the hope of an armed intervention in favour of their
independence. In such conditions, judging from the
ordinary narrow military standpoint, to destroy the
Bank of Russia and several Ministries, and to spread a
panic in the capital might have been considered a good
plan of warfare; but there never was the slightest
scrap of evidence forthcoming to support this hypothesis.

On the other side, the advanced parties in Russia
saw that no hope could any longer be placed in
Alexander's reformatory initiative: he was clearly

drifting into the reactionary camp. To men of fore-
thought it was evident that the liberation of the serfs,
under the conditions of redemption which were imposed
upon them, meant their certain ruin, and revolutionary
proclamations were issued in May at St. Petersburg
calling the people and the army to a general revolt,
while the educated classes were asked to insist upon
the necessity of a National Convention. Under such
circumstances, to disorganize the machine of the
government might have entered into the plans of some
revolutionists.

Finally, the indefinite character of the emancipation had produced a great deal of fermentation among
the peasants, who constitute a considerable part of the
population in all Russian cities; and through all the
history of Russia, every time such a fermentation has
begun it has resulted in anonymous letters foretelling
fires, and eventually in incendiarism.

It was possible that the idea of setting the Apráxin
market on fire might occur to isolated men in the
revolutionary camp, but neither the most searching
inquiries nor the wholesale arrests which began all
over Russia and Poland immediately after the fire
revealed the slightest indication showing that such was
really the case. If anything of the sort had been
found, the reactionary party would have made capital
out of it. Many reminiscences and volumes of correspondence from those times have since been published,
but they contain no hint whatever in support of this
suspicion.

On the contrary, when similar conflagrations broke
out in several towns on the Vólga, and especially at

Sarátoff, and when Zhdánoff, a member of the Senate, was sent by the Tsar to make a searching inquiry, he returned with the firm conviction that the conflagration at Sarátoff was the work of the reactionary party. There was among that party a general belief that it would be possible to induce Alexander II. to postpone the final abolition of serfdom, which was to take place on February 19, 1863. They knew the weakness of his character, and immediately after the great fire at St. Petersburg they began a violent campaign for postponement, and for the revision of the emancipation law in its practical applications. It was rumoured in well-informed legal circles that Senator Zhdánoff was in fact returning with positive proofs of the culpability of the reactionaries at Sarátoff; but he died on his way back, his portfolio disappeared, and it has never been found.

Be it as it may, the Apráxin fire had the most deplorable consequences. After it Alexander II. surrendered to the reactionaries, and—what was still worse—the public opinion of that part of society at St. Petersburg, and especially at Moscow, which carried most weight with the government suddenly threw off its liberal garb, and turned against not only the more advanced section of the reform party, but even against its moderate wing. A few days after the conflagration I went on Sunday to see my cousin, the aide-de-camp of the emperor, in whose apartment I had often heard the Horse Guard officers expressing sympathy with Chernyshévsky; my cousin himself had been up till then an assiduous reader of 'The Contemporary' (the organ of the advanced reform party). Now he brought several

numbers of 'The Contemporary,' and, putting them on
the table I was sitting at, said to me : ' Well, now, after
this I will have no more of that incendiary stuff;
enough of it '—and these words expressed the opinion
of ' all St. Petersburg.' It became improper to talk of
reforms. The whole atmosphere was laden with a
reactionary spirit. 'The Contemporary' and other
similar reviews were suppressed; the Sunday schools
were prohibited under any form; wholesale arrests
began. The capital was placed under a state of siege.

A fortnight later, on June 13 (25), the time which
we pages and cadets had so long looked for came at
last. The emperor gave us a sort of military examina-
tion in all kinds of evolutions—during which we commanded the companies and I paraded on a horse before
the battalion—and we were promoted to be officers.

When the parade was over, Alexander II. loudly
called out, ' The promoted officers to me ! ' and we
gathered round him. He remained on horseback.

Here I saw him in a quite new light. The man
who the next year appeared in the *rôle* of a blood-
thirsty and vindictive suppressor of the insurrection in
Poland rose now, full size, before my eyes, in the
speech he addressed to us.

He began in a quiet tone. 'I congratulate you :
you are officers.' He spoke about military duty and
loyalty as they are usually spoken of on such occasions.
' But if any one of you,' he went on, distinctly shouting
out every word, his face suddenly contorted with anger,
' but if any one of you—which God preserve you
from—should under any circumstances prove disloyal

to the Tsar, the throne, and the fatherland—take heed of what I say—he will be treated with all the se-ve-ri-ty of the laws, without the slightest com-mi-se-ra-tion! '

His voice failed; his face was peevish, full of that expression of blind rage which I saw in my childhood on the faces of landlords when they threatened their serfs ' to skin them under the rods.' He violently spurred his horse, and rode out of our circle. Next morning, June 14, by his orders three officers were shot at Módlin in Poland, and one soldier, Szur by name, was killed under the rods.

' Reaction, full speed backwards,' I said to myself as we made our way back to the corps.

I saw Alexander II. once more before leaving St. Petersburg. Some days after our promotion, all the newly appointed officers were at the palace, to be presented to, him. My more than modest uniform, with its prominent grey trousers, attracted universal attention, and every moment I had to satisfy the curiosity of officers of all ranks, who came to ask me what was the uniform that I wore. The Amúr Cossacks being then the youngest regiment of the Russian army, I stood somewhere near the end of the hundreds of officers who were present. Alexander II. found me and asked, ' So you go to Siberia? Did your father consent to it, after all ? ' I answered in the affirmative. ' Are you not afraid to go so far ? ' I warmly replied : ' No, I want to work. There must be so much to do in Siberia to apply the great reforms which are going to be made.' He looked straight at me ; he became

pensive; at last he said, 'Well, go; one can be useful
everywhere;' and his face took on such an expression
of fatigue, such a character of complete surrender, that
I thought at once, 'He is a used-up man; he is going
to give it all up.'

St. Petersburg had assumed a gloomy aspect. Soldiers marched in the streets. Cossack patrols rode
round the palace, the fortress was filled with prisoners.
Wherever I went I saw the same thing—the triumph
of the reaction. I left St. Petersburg without regret.

I went every day to the Cossack administration to
ask them to make haste and deliver me my papers,
and as soon as they were ready I hurried to Moscow
to join my brother Alexander.

II

THE five years that I spent in Siberia were for me a
genuine education in life and human character. I was
brought into contact with men of all descriptions: the
best and the worst; those who stood at the top of society
and those who vegetated at the very bottom — the
tramps and the so-called incorrigible criminals. I had
ample opportunities to watch the ways and habits of
the peasants in their daily life, and still more opportunities to appreciate how little the State administration
could give to them, even if it were animated by the
very best intentions. Finally, my extensive journeys,
during which I travelled over fifty thousand miles in

carts, on board steamers, in boats, but chiefly on horseback, had a wonderful effect in strengthening my health. They also taught me how little man really needs as soon as he comes out of the enchanted circle of conventional civilization. With a few pounds of bread and a few ounces of tea in a leather bag, a kettle and a hatchet hanging at the side of the saddle, and under the saddle a blanket, to be spread at the camp fire upon a bed of freshly cut spruce twigs, a man feels wonderfully independent, even amidst unknown mountains thickly clothed with woods or capped with snow. A book might be written about this part of my life, but I must rapidly glide over it here, there being so much more to say about the later periods.

Siberia is not the frozen land buried in snow and peopled with exiles only that it is imagined to be, even by many Russians. In its southern parts it is as rich in natural productions as are the southern parts of Canada, which it resembles very much in its physical aspects; and beside half a million of natives, it has a population of more than four millions of Russians. The southern parts of West Siberia are as thoroughly Russian as the provinces to the north of Moscow.

In 1862 the upper administration of Siberia was far more enlightened and far better all round than that of any province of Russia proper. For several years the post of Governor-General of East Siberia had been occupied by a remarkable personage, Count N. N. Muravióff, who annexed the Amúr region to Russia. He was very intelligent, very active, extremely amiable, and desirous to work for the good of the country. Like all men of action of the governmental school, he

was a despot at the bottom of his heart; but he held
advanced opinions, and a democratic republic would
not have quite satisfied him.   He had succeeded to a
great extent in getting rid of the old staff of civil service
officials, who considered Siberia a camp to be plundered,
and he had gathered around him a number of young
officials, quite honest, and many of them animated by
the same excellent intentions as himself.   In his own
study, the young officers, with the exile Bakúnin
among them (he escaped from Siberia in the autumn
of 1861), discussed the chances of creating the United
States of Siberia, federated across the· Pacific Ocean
with the United States of America.

When I came to Irkútsk, the capital of East Siberia,
the wave of reaction which I saw rising at St. Petersburg had not yet reached these distant dominions.   I
was very well received by the young Governor-General,
Korsákoff, who had just succeeded Muravióff, and he
told me that he was delighted to have about him men
of liberal opinions.   As to the commander of the General
Staff, Kúkel—a young general not yet thirty-five years
old, whose personal aide-de-camp I became—he at
once took me to a room in his house, where I found,
together with the best Russian reviews, complete
collections of the London revolutionary editions of
Hérzen.   We were soon warm friends.

General Kúkel temporarily occupied at that time
the post of Governor of Transbaikália, and a few weeks
later we crossed the beautiful Lake Baikál and went
further east, to the little town of Chitá, the capital of
the province.   There I had to give myself, heart and

soul, without loss of time, to the great reforms which were then under discussion. The St. Petersburg Ministries had applied to the local authorities, asking them to work out schemes of complete reform in the administration of the provinces, the organization of the police, the tribunals, the prisons, the system of exile, the self-government of the townships—all on broadly liberal bases laid down by the emperor in his manifestoes.

Kúkel, supported by an intelligent and practical man, Colonel Pedashénko, and by a couple of well-meaning civil service officials, worked all day long, and often a good deal of the night. I became the secretary of two committees—for the reform of the prisons and the whole system of exile, and for preparing a scheme of municipal self-government—and I set to work with all the enthusiasm of a youth of nineteen years. I read much about the historical development of these institutions in Russia and their present condition abroad, excellent works and papers dealing with these subjects having been published by the Ministries of the Interior and of Justice; but what we did in Transbaikália was by no means merely theoretical. I discussed first the general outlines, and subsequently every point of detail, with practical men, well acquainted with the real needs and the local possibilities; and for that purpose I met a considerable number of men both in town and in the province. Then the conclusions we arrived at were re-discussed with Kúkel and Pedashénko; and when I had put the results into a preliminary shape, every point was again very thoroughly thrashed out in the committees. One of these committees, for preparing the municipal government scheme, was composed of citizens of Chitá, elected by all the population, as freely as they might have been elected in the United States. In short, our work was very serious; and even now, looking back at it through the perspective of so many years, I can say in full confidence that if municipal self-government had been granted then, in the modest shape which we gave to it, the towns of Siberia would be very different from what they are. But nothing came of it all, as will presently be seen.

There was no lack of other incidental occupations. Money had to be found for the support of charitable institutions; an economic description of the province had to be written in connection with a local agricultural exhibition; or some serious inquiry had to be made. 'It is a great epoch we live in; work, my dear friend; remember that you are the secretary of all existing and future committees,' Kúkel would sometimes say to me, —and I worked with doubled energy.

One example or two will show with what results. There was in our province a ' district chief '—that is, a police officer invested with very wide and indeterminate rights—who was simply a disgrace. He robbed the peasants and flogged them right and left—even women, which was against the law; and when a criminal affair fell into his hands, it might lie there for months, men being kept in the meantime in prison till they gave him a bribe. Kúkel would have dismissed this man long before, but the Governor-General did not like the idea of it, because he had strong protectors at St. Petersburg. After much hesitation, it was decided

at last that I should go to make an investigation on
the spot, and collect evidence against the man. This
was not by any means easy, because the peasants,
terrorized by him, and well knowing an old Russian
saying, 'God is far away, while your chief is your
next-door neighbour,' did not dare to testify. Even
the woman he had flogged was afraid at first to make
a written statement. It was only after I had stayed a
fortnight with the peasants, and had won their confidence, that the misdeeds of their chief could be
brought to light. I collected crushing evidence, and
the district chief was dismissed. We congratulated ourselves on having got rid of such a pest. What was,
however, our astonishment when, a few months later,
we learned that this same man had been nominated to
a higher post in Kamchátka ! There he could plunder
the natives free of any control, and so he did. A few
years later he returned to St. Petersburg a rich man.
The articles he occasionally contributes now to the
reactionary press are, as one might expect, full of high
' patriotic ' spirit.

The wave of reaction, as I have already said, had
not then reached Siberia, and the political exiles continued to be treated with all possible leniency, as in
Muravióff's time. When, in 1861, the poet Mikháiloff
was condemned to hard labour for a revolutionary pro-
clamation which he had issued, and was sent to Siberia,
the Governor of the first Siberian town on his way,
Tobólsk, gave a dinner in his honour, in which all the
officials took part. In Transbaikália he was not kept
at hard labour, but was allowed officially to stay in the
hospital prison of a small mining village. His health

being very poor—he was dying from consumption, and did actually die a few months later—General Kúkel gave him permission to stay in the house of his brother, a mining engineer, who had rented a gold mine from the Crown on his own account. Unofficially that was well known in East Siberia. But one day we learned from Irkútsk that, in consequence of a secret denunciation, a General of the gendarmes (state police) was on his way to Chitá to make a strict inquiry into the affair. An aide-de-camp of the Governor-General brought us the news. I was despatched in great haste to warn Mikháiloff, and to tell him that he must return at once to the hospital prison, while the General of the gendarmes was kept at Chitá. As that gentleman found himself every night the winner of considerable sums of money at the green table in Kúkel's house, he soon decided not to exchange this pleasant pastime for a long journey to the mines in a temperature which was then a dozen degrees below the freezing-point of mercury, and eventually went back to Irkútsk quite satisfied with his lucrative mission.

The storm, however, was coming nearer and nearer, and it swept everything before it soon after the insurrection broke out in Poland.

III

In January 1863 Poland rose against Russian rule. Insurrectionary bands were formed, and a war began which lasted for full eighteen months. The London refugees had implored the Polish revolutionary committees to postpone the movement. They foresaw that it would be crushed, and would put an end to the reform period in Russia. But it could not be helped. The repression of the nationalist manifestations which took place at Warsaw in 1861, and the cruel, quite unprovoked executions which followed, exasperated the Poles. The die was cast.

Never before had the Polish cause so many sympathizers in Russia as at that time. I do not speak of the revolutionists; but even among the more moderate elements of Russian society it was thought, and was openly said, that it would be a benefit for Russia to have in Poland a friendly neighbour instead of a hostile subject. Poland will never lose her national character, it is too strongly developed; she has, and will have, her own literature, her own art and industry. Russia can keep her in servitude only by means of sheer force and oppression—a condition of things which has hitherto favoured, and necessarily will favour, oppression in Russia herself. Even the peaceful Slavophiles were of that opinion; and while I was at school St. Petersburg society greeted with full approval the 'dream' which the Slavophile Iván Aksákoff had the courage to print in his paper, ' The Day.' His dream was that the Russian troops had evacuated Poland, and he discussed the excellent results which would follow.

When the revolution of 1863 broke out, several Russian officers refused to march against the Poles, while others openly took their part, and died either on the scaffold or on the battlefield. Funds for the insurrection were collected all over Russia—quite openly in Siberia—and in the Russian universities the students equipped those of their comrades who were going to join the revolutionists.

Then, amidst this effervescence, the news spread over Russia that during the night of January 10 bands of insurgents had fallen upon the soldiers who were cantoned in the villages, and had murdered them in their beds, although on the very eve of that day the relations of the troops with the Poles seemed to be quite friendly. There was some exaggeration in the report, but unfortunately there was also truth in it, and the impression it produced in Russia was most disastrous. The old antipathies between the two nations, so akin in their origins but so different in their national characters, woke up once more.

Gradually the bad feeling faded away to some extent. The gallant fight of the always brave sons of Poland, and the indomitable energy with which they resisted a formidable army, won sympathy for that heroic nation. But it became known that the Polish revolutionary committee, in its demand for the re-establishment of Poland with its old frontiers, included the Little Russian or Ukraïnian provinces, the Greek Orthodox population of which hated their Polish rulers, and more than once in the course of the last three centuries slaughtered them wholesale. Moreover, Napoleon III. began to menace Russia with a new war —a vain menace, which did more harm to the Poles than all other things put together. And finally, the radical elements of Russia saw with regret that now the purely nationalist elements of Poland had got the upper hand, the revolutionary government did not care in the least to grant the land to the serfs—a blunder of which the Russian government did not fail to take advantage, in order to appear in the position of protector of the peasants against their Polish landlords.

When the revolution broke out in Poland it was generally believed in Russia that it would take a democratic, republican turn ; and that the liberation of the serfs on a broad democratic basis would be the first thing which a revolutionary government, fighting for the independence of the country, would accomplish.

The Emancipation Law, as it had been enacted at St. Petersburg in 1861, provided ample opportunity for such a course of action. The personal obligations of the serfs towards their owners only came to an end on February 19, 1863. Then a very slow process had to be gone through in order to obtain a sort of agreement between the landlords and the serfs as to the size and the locality of the land allotments which were to be given to the liberated serfs. The yearly payments for these allotments (disproportionately high) were fixed by law at so much per acre ; but the peasants had also to pay an additional sum for their homesteads, and of this sum the maximum only had been fixed by the statute—it having been thought that the landlords might be induced to forgo that additional payment, or to be satisfied with only a part of it. As to the so-called 'redemption' of the land—in which case the Government undertook to pay the landlord its full value in State bonds and the peasants receiving the land had to pay in return, for forty-nine years, six per cent. on that sum as interest and annuities—not only were these payments extravagant and ruinous for the peasants, but no term

was even fixed for the redemption : it was left to
the will of the landlord ; and in an immense number
of cases the redemption arrangements had not been
entered upon twenty years after the emancipation.

Under such conditions a revolutionary government
had ample opportunity for immensely improving upon
the Russian law.   It was bound to accomplish an
act of justice towards the serfs—whose condition in
Poland was as bad as, and often worse than, in
Russia itself—by granting them better and more
definite conditions of emancipation.   But nothing of
the sort was done.   The purely nationalist party and
the aristocratic one having obtained the upper hand
in the movement, this all-absorbing matter was left out
of sight.   It was thus easy for the Russian Government to win the peasants to its side.

Full advantage was taken of this fault when
Nicholas Milútin was sent to Poland by Alexander II.
with the mission to liberate the peasants in the way
he intended doing it in Russia.   ' Go to Poland ;
apply there your Red programme against the Polish
landlords,' said Alexander II. to him ; and Milútin, together with Prince Cherkássky and many others, really
did their best to take the land from the landlords and
give full-sized allotments to the peasants.

I once met one of the Russian functionaries who
went to Poland under Milútin and Prince Cherkássky.
' We had full liberty,' he said to me, ' to hold out the
hand to the peasants.   My usual plan was to go to a
village and convoke the peasants' assembly.   " Tell me
first," I would say, "what land do you hold at this

moment ? " They would point it out to me. " Is this
all the land you ever held ? " I would then ask. " Surely
not," they would reply with one voice; "years ago
these meadows were ours; this wood was once in our
possession; and these fields belonged to us." I would
let them go on talking it all over, and then would
ask : " Now, which of you can certify under oath that
this land or that land has ever been held by you ? " Of
course there would be nobody forthcoming—it was
all too long ago. At last, some old man would be thrust
out from the crowd, the rest saying : " He knows all
about it, he can swear to it." The old man would begin
a long story about what he knew in his youth, or had
heard from his father, but I would cut the story
short. . . . " State on oath what you know to have been
held by the *gmina* (the village community)—and the land
is yours." And as soon as he took the oath—one could
trust that oath implicitly—I wrote out the papers and
declared to the assembly : " Now, this land is yours.
You stand no longer under any obligations whatever to
your late masters : you are simply their neighbours;
all you will have to do is to pay the redemption tax, so
much every year, to the Government. Your homesteads
go with the land : you get them free." '

One can imagine the effect which such a policy
produced upon the peasants. A cousin of mine, Petr
Nikoláevich, a brother of the aide-de-camp whom I have
mentioned, was in Poland or in Lithuania with his
regiment of uhlans of the Guard. The revolution was
so serious that even the regiments of the Guard had been
sent against it from St. Petersburg; and it is now
known that when Mikhael Muravióff was ordered to

Lithuania, and came to take leave of the Empress Marie, she said to him : ' Save at least Lithuania for Russia.' Poland was regarded as lost.

'The armed bands of the revolutionists held the country,' my cousin said to me, ' and we were powerless to defeat them, or even to find them. Small bands over and over again attacked our small detachments, and as they fought admirably, and knew the country and found support in the population, they often had the best of the skirmishes. We were thus compelled to march in large columns only. We would cross a region, marching through the woods without finding any trace of the bands ; but when we marched back again we learned that bands had appeared in our rear, that they had levied the patriotic tax in the country, and if some peasant had rendered himself useful in any way to our troops we found him hanged on a tree by the revolutionary bands. So it went on for months, with no chance of improvement, until Milútin came and freed the peasants, giving them the land. Then—all was over. The peasants sided with us ; they helped us to lay hold of the bands, and the insurrection came to an end.'

I often spoke with the Polish exiles in Siberia upon this subject, and some of them understood the fault that had been committed. A revolution, from its very outset, must be an act of justice towards the ' down-trodden and the oppressed '—not a promise of making such reparation later on—otherwise it is sure to fail. Unfortunately, it often happens that the leaders are so much absorbed with mere questions of military tactics that they forget the main thing. To be revolutionists, and fail to prove to the masses that a new era has really begun for them, is to ensure the certain ruin of the attempt.

The disastrous consequences for Poland of this revolution are known ; they belong to the domain of history. How many thousand men perished in battle, how many hundreds were hanged, and how many scores of thousands were transported to various provinces of Russia and Siberia, is not yet fully known. But even the official figures which were printed in Russia a few years ago show that in the Lithuanian provinces alone —not to speak of Poland proper—that terrible man Mikhael Muravióff, to whom the Russian Government has just erected a monument at Wílno, hanged by his own authority 128 Poles, and transported to Russia and Siberia 9,423 men and women. Official lists, also published in Russia, give 18,672 men and women exiled to Siberia from Poland, of whom 10,407 were sent to East Siberia. I remember that the Governor-General of East Siberia mentioned to me the same number, about 11,000 persons, sent to hard labour or exile in his domains. I saw them there, and witnessed their sufferings. Altogether, something like 60,000 or 70,000 persons, if not more, were torn out of Poland and transported to different provinces of Russia, to the Urals, to Caucasus, and to Siberia.

For Russia the consequences were equally disastrous. The Polish insurrection was the definitive close of the reform period. True, the law of provincial self-government (*Zémstvos*) and the reform of the law courts were promulgated in 1864 and 1866 ; but both were ready in 1862, and, moreover, at the last moment Alexander II. gave preference to the scheme of self-government

which had been prepared by the reactionary party of
Valúeff, as against the scheme which had been prepared by Nicholas Milútin ; and immediately after the
promulgation of both reforms their importance was
reduced, and in some cases destroyed, by the enactment
of a number of by-laws.

Worst of all, public opinion itself took a further step
backward.   The hero of the hour was Katkóff, the
leader of the serfdom party, who appeared now as a
Russian 'patriot,' and carried with him most of the St.
Petersburg and Moscow society.   After that time, those
who dared to speak of reforms were at once classed by
Katkóff as ' traitors to Russia.'

The wave of reaction soon reached our remote
province.   One day in March a paper was brought by
a special messenger from Irkútsk.   It intimated to
General Kúkel that he was at once to leave the post of
Governor of Transbaikália and go to Irkútsk, waiting
there for further orders, but without reassuming
there the post of commander of the general staff.

Why ?   What did that mean ?   There was not a
word of explanation.   Even the Governor-General, a
personal friend of Kúkel, had not run the risk of adding
a single word to the mysterious order.   Did it mean
that Kúkel was going to be taken between two
gendarmes to St. Petersburg, and immured in that
huge stone coffin, the fortress of St. Peter and St. Paul ?
All was possible.   Later on we learned that such was
indeed the intention ; and so it would have been done
but for the energetic intervention of Count Nicholas
Muravióff, ' the conqueror of the Amúr,' who personally

implored the Tsar that Kúkel should be spared that fate.

Our parting with Kúkel and his charming family was like a funeral. My heart was very heavy. I not only lost in him a dear personal friend, but I felt also that this parting was the burial of a whole epoch, full of long-cherished hopes—'full of illusions,' as it became the fashion to say.

So it was. A new Governor came—a good-natured, 'leave-me-in-peace' man. With renewed energy, seeing that there was no time to lose, I completed our plans of reform of the system of exile and municipal self-government. The Governor made a few objections here and there for formality's sake, but finally signed the schemes, and they were sent to headquarters. But at St. Petersburg reforms were no longer wanted. There our projects lie buried still, with hundreds of similar ones from all parts of Russia. A few 'improved' prisons, even more terrible than the old unimproved ones, have been built in the capitals, to be shown during prison congresses to distinguished foreigners; but the remainder, and the whole system of exile, were found by George Kennan in 1886 in exactly the same state in which I left them in 1862. Only now, after thirty-six years have passed away, the authorities are introducing the reformed tribunals and a parody of self-government in Siberia, and committees have been nominated again to inquire into the system of exile.

When Kennan came back to London from his journey to Siberia he managed, on the very next day after his arrival in London, to hunt up Stepniák, Tchaykóvsky, myself, and another Russian refugee. In the evening we all met at Kennan's room in a small hotel near Charing Cross. We saw him for the first time, and having no excess of confidence in enterprising Englishmen who had previously undertaken to learn all about the Siberian prisons without even learning a word of Russian, we began to cross-examine Kennan. To our astonishment, he not only spoke excellent Russian, but he knew everything worth knowing about Siberia. One or another of us had been acquainted with the greater proportion of all political exiles in Siberia, and we besieged Kennan with questions: 'Where is So-and-So? Is he married? Is he happy in his marriage? Does he still keep fresh in spirit?' We were soon satisfied that Kennan knew all about every one of them.

When this questioning was over, and we were preparing to leave, I asked, ' Do you know, Mr. Kennan, if they have built a watchtower for the fire brigade at Chitá?' Stepniák looked at me, as if to reproach me for abusing Kennan's good will. Kennan, however, began to laugh, and I soon joined him. And with much laughter we tossed each other questions and answers: 'Why, do you know about that?' 'And you too?' 'Built?' 'Yes, double estimates!' and so on, till at last Stepniák interfered, and in his most severely good-natured way objected: 'Tell us at least what you are laughing about.' Whereupon Kennan told the story of that watchtower which his readers must remember. In 1859 the Chitá people wanted to build a watchtower, and collected the money for it; but their estimates had to be sent to the Ministry of the Interior. So they went to St. Petersburg; but when they came back, two years later, duly approved, all the prices for timber and work had gone up in that rising young town.   This was in 1862, while I was at Chitá.   New estimates were made and sent to St. Petersburg, and the story was repeated for full twenty-five years, till at last the Chitá people, losing patience, put in their estimates prices nearly double the real ones. These fantastic estimates were solemnly considered at St. Petersburg, and approved.   This is how Chitá got its watchtower.

It has often been said that Alexander II. committed a great fault, and brought about his own ruin, by raising so many hopes which later on he did not satisfy. It is seen from what I have just said—and the story of little Chitá was the story of all Russia—that he did worse than that.   It was not merely that he raised hopes.   Yielding for a moment to the current of public opinion around him, he induced men all over Russia to set to work, to issue from the domain of mere hopes and dreams, ånd to touch with the finger the reforms that were required.   He made them realize what could be done immediately, and how easy it was to do it ; he induced them to sacrifice whatever of their ideals could not be immediately realized, and to demand only what was practically possible at the time.   And when they had framed their ideas, and had shaped them into laws which merely required his signature to become realities, then he refused that signature.   No reactionist could raise, or ever has raised, his voice to assert that what was left—the unreformed tribunals, the absence of municipal government, or the system of exile—was good and was worth maintaining : no one has dared to

say that.   And yet, owing to the fear of doing anything,
all was left as it was ; for thirty-five years those who
ventured to mention the necessity of a change were
treated as ' suspects ; ' and institutions unanimously
recognized as bad were permitted to continue in existence only that nothing more might be heard of that
abhorred word ' reform.'

IV

SEEING that there was nothing more to be done at
Chitá in the way of reforms, I gladly accepted the
offer to visit the Amúr that same summer of 1863.

The immense domain on the left (northern) bank of
the Amúr, and along the Pacific Coast as far south as
the Bay of Peter the Great (Vladivostók), had been
annexed to Russia by Count Muravióff, almost against
the will of the St. Petersburg authorities and certainly
without much help from them.   When he conceived
the bold plan of taking possession of the great river
whose southern position and fertile lands had for the
last two hundred years always attracted the Siberians ;
and when, on the eve of the opening of Japan to
Europe, he decided to take for Russia a strong position
on the Pacific coast and to join hands with the United
States, he had almost everybody against him at
St. Petersburg : the Ministry of War, which had no
men to dispose of, the Ministry of Finance, which had
no money for annexations, and especially the Ministry

of Foreign Affairs, always guided by its pre-occupation
of avoiding ' diplomatic complications.'   Muravióff had
thus to act on his own responsibility, and to rely upon
the scanty means which thinly populated Eastern
Siberia could afford for this grand enterprise.   Moreover, everything had to be done in a hurry, in order to
oppose the ' accomplished fact ' to the protests of the
West European diplomatists, which would certainly
be raised.

A nominal occupation would have been of no avail,
and the idea was to have on the whole length of the
great river and of its southern tributary, the Usurí—
full 2,500 miles—a chain of self-supporting settlements, and thus to establish a regular communication
between Siberia and the Pacific Coast.   Men were
wanted for these settlements, and as the scanty population of East Siberia could not supply them, Muravióff
did not recoil before any kind of means of getting men.
Released convicts who, after having served their time,
had become serfs to the Imperial mines, were freed and
organized as Transbaikálian Cossacks, part of whom
were settled along the Amúr and the Usurí, forming
two new Cossack communities.   Then Muraviótf
obtained the release of a thousand hard-labour convicts
(mostly robbers and murderers), who had to be settled
as free men on the lower Amúr.   He came himself to
see them off, and, as they were going to leave, addressed
them on the beach : ' Go, my children, be free there,
cultivate the land, make it Russian soil, start a new
life,' and so on.   The Russian peasant women nearly
always follow, of their own free will, their husbands if
the latter happen to be sent to hard labour to Siberia,

and many of the would-be colonists had their families with them. But those who had none ventured to remark to Muravióff : 'What is agriculture without a wife? We ought to be married.' Whereupon Muravióff ordered to release all the hard-labour convict women of the place—about a hundred—and offered them the choice of the man each of them would like to marry and to follow. However, there was little time to lose; the high water in the river was rapidly going down, the rafts had to start, and Muravióff, asking the people to stand in pairs on the beach, blessed them, saying : 'I marry you, children. Be kind to each other; you men, don't ill-treat your wives—and be happy ! '

I saw these settlers some six years after that scene. Their villages were poor, the land they had been settled on having had to be cleared from under virgin forests ; but, all taken, their settlements were not a failure, and 'the Muravióff marriages' were not less happy than marriages are on the average. That excellent, intelligent man, Innocentus, bishop of the Amúr, recognized, later on, these marriages, as well as the children which were born, as quite legal, and had them inscribed on the Church registers.

Muravióff was less successful, though, with another batch of men that he added to the population of East Siberia. In his penury of men he had accepted a couple of thousand soldiers from the punishment battalions. They were incorporated as ' adopted sons ' in the families of the Cossacks, or were settled in joint households in the villages. But ten or twenty years of barrack life under the horrid discipline of Nicholas I.'s time surely was not a preparation for an agricultural life. The 'sons' deserted their adopted fathers and constituted the floating population of the towns, living from hand to mouth on occasional jobs, spending chiefly in drink what they earned, and then again living as birds in the sky in the expectation of another job turning up.

The motley crowd of Transbaikálian Cossacks, of ex-convicts, and ' sons,' who were settled in a hurry and often in a haphazard way along the banks of the Amúr, certainly did not attain prosperity, especially in the lower parts of the river and on the Usurí, where every square yard had often to be won upon a virgin sub-tropical forest, and deluges of rain brought by the monsoons in July, inundations on a gigantic scale, millions of migrating birds, and the like continually destroyed the crops, finally bringing whole populations to sheer despair and apathy.

Considerable supplies of salt, flour, cured meat, and so on had thus to be shipped every year to support both the regular troops and the settlements on the lower Amúr, and for that purpose some hundred and fifty barges used to be built and loaded at Chitá, and floated with the early spring floods down the Ingodá, the Shílka, and the Amúr. The whole flotilla was divided into detachments of from twenty to thirty barges, which were placed under the orders of a number of Cossack and civil-service officers. Most of them did not know much about navigation, but they could be trusted, at least, not to steal the provisions and then report them as lost. I was nominated assistant to the chief of all that flotilla—let me name him, Major Maróvsky.

My first experiences in my new capacity of
navigator were all but successful. It so happened that
I had to proceed with a few barges as rapidly as
possible to a certain point on the Amúr, and there to
hand over my vessels. For that purpose I had to hire
men exactly from among those 'sons' whom I have
already mentioned. None of them had ever had any
experience in river navigation, nor had I. On the
morning of our start my crew had to be collected from
the public houses of the place, most of them being so
drunk at that early hour that they had to be bathed
in the river to bring them back to their senses.
When we were afloat, I had to teach them everything
that had to be done. Still, things went pretty well
during the day; the barges, carried along by a swift
current, floated down the river, and my crew, inexpe-
rienced though they were, had no interest in throwing
their vessels upon the shore—that would have required
special exertion. But when dusk came, and our huge
heavily laden fifty-ton barges had to be brought to the
shore and fastened to it for the night, one of the barges,
which was far ahead of the one upon which I was, was
stopped only when it was fast upon a rock, at the foot
of a tremendously high inaccessible cliff. There it
stood immovable, while the level of the river, temporarily swollen by rains, was rapidly going down. My
ten men evidently could not move it. So I rowed down
to the next village to ask assistance from the Cossacks,
and at the same time despatched a messenger to a friend
—a Cossack officer who stayed some twenty miles away
and who had experience in such things.

The morning came; a hundred Cossacks—men and

women—had come to my aid, but there was no means whatever to connect the barge with the shore, in order to unload it—so deep was the water under the cliff. And, as soon as we attempted to push it off the rock, its bottom was broken in and water freely entered it, sweeping away the flour and the salt of the cargo. To my great horror, I perceived lots of small fish entering through the hole and freely swimming about in the barge—and I stood there helpless, not knowing what to do next. There is a very simple and effective remedy for such emergencies. A sack of flour is thrust into the hole, and it soon takes its shape, while the outer crust of paste which is formed in the sack prevents water from penetrating through the flour; but none of us knew anything about it. Happily enough, a few minutes later a barge was signalled coming down the river towards us. The appearance of the swan who carried Lohengrin was not greeted with more enthusiasm by the despairing Elsa than that clumsy vessel was greeted by me. The haze which covered the beautiful Shílka at that early hour in the morning added even more to the poetry of the vision. It was my friend the Cossack officer, who had realized by my description that no human force could drag my barge off the rock—that it was lost—and taking an empty barge which by chance was at hand, came with it to place upon it the cargo of my doomed craft. Now the hole was filled up, the water was pumped out, and the cargo was transferred to the new barge, which was fastened alongside mine; and next morning I could continue my journey. This little experience was of great profit to me, and I soon reached my destination on the Amúr without further adventures worth mentioning. Every night we found out some stretch of steep but relatively low shore where to stop with the barges for the night, and our fires were soon lighted on the bank of the swift and clear river, amidst most beautiful mountain scenery. In daytime, one could hardly imagine a more pleasant journey than on board a barge which leisurely floats down, without any of the noises of a steamer— one or two strokes being occasionally given with its immense stern rudder to keep it in the main current. For the lover of nature, the lower part of the Shílka and the upper part of the Amúr, where one sees a most beautiful, wide, and swift river flowing amidst mountains rising in steep wooded cliffs a couple of thousand feet above the water, offers one of the most delightful scenes in the world. But on that very account communication along the shore, on horseback, along a narrow trail, is extremely difficult. I learned this that same autumn at my own expense. In East Siberia the seven last stations along the Shílka (about 120 miles) were known as the Seven Mortal Sins. This stretch of the Trans-Siberian railway—if it is ever built—will cost unimaginable sums of money: much more than the stretch of the Canadian Pacific line in the Rocky Mountains, in the Canyon of the Fraser River, has cost.

After I had delivered my barges, I made about a thousand miles down the Amúr in one of the post boats which are used on the river. The boat is covered with a light shed in its back part, and has on its stem a box filled with earth upon which a fire is kept to cook the food. My crew consisted of three men. We had to

make haste, and therefore used to row in turns all day
long, while at night the boat was left to float with the
current, and I kept the watch for three or four hours
to maintain the boat in the midst of the river and to
prevent it from being dragged into some side branch.
These watches—the full moon shining above, and the
dark hills reflected in the river—were beautiful beyond
description. My rowers were taken from the same
'sons;' they were three tramps who had the reputation
of being incorrigible thieves and robbers—and I carried
with me a heavy sack full of bank-notes, silver, and
copper. In Western Europe such a journey on a
lonely river would have been considered risky—not so in
East Siberia; I made it without even having so much
as an old pistol, and I found my three tramps excellent
company. Only as we approached Blagovéschensk
they became restless. 'Khánshina' (the Chinese
brandy) is cheap there,' they reasoned with deep sighs.
'We are sure to get into trouble! It's cheap, and it
knocks you over in no time from want of being used to
it!' . . . I offered to leave the money which was due
to them with a friend, who would see them off with
the first steamer. 'That would not help us,' they
replied mournfully; 'somebody will offer a glass . . .
it's cheap, . . . and a glass knocks you over!' they
persisted in saying. They were really perplexed, and
when, a few months later, I returned through the town
I learned that one of 'my sons'—as people called
them in town—had really got into trouble. When he
had sold the last pair of boots to get the poisonous drink,
he had made some theft and was locked up. My friend
finally obtained his release and shipped him back.

Only those who have seen the Amúr, or know the Mississippi or the Yang-tse-kiang, can imagine what an immense river the Amúr becomes after it has joined the Sungarí and can realize what tremendous waves roll up its bed if the weather is stormy. When the rainy season, due to the monsoons, comes in July, the Sungarí, the Usurí, and the Amúr are swollen by unimaginable quantities of water; thousands of low islands, usually covered with willow thickets, are inundated or torn away, and the width of the river attains in places two, three, and even five miles; water rushes into hundreds of branches and lakes which spread in the lowlands along the main channel; and when a fresh wind blows from an eastern quarter, against the current, tremendous waves, higher than those which one sees in the estuary of the St. Lawrence, roll up the main channel as well as up its branches. Still worse is it when a typhoon blows from the Chinese Sea and spreads over the Amúr region.

We experienced such a typhoon. I was then on board a large decked boat, with Major Maróvsky, whom I had joined at Blagovéschensk. He had well provided his boat with sails, which permitted us to sail close to the wind, and when the storm began we managed, nevertheless, to bring our boat on the sheltered side of the river and to find refuge in some small tributary. There we stayed for two days while the storm raged with such fury that when I ventured for a few hundred yards into the surrounding forest, I had to retreat on account of the number of immense trees which the wind was blowing down round me. We began to feel very uneasy for our barges. It was evident that if they had been afloat this morning, they never would have been able to reach the sheltered side of the river, but must have been driven by the storm to the bank exposed to the full rage of the wind, and there they must have been destroyed. A disaster was almost certain.

We sailed out as soon as the main fury of the storm had abated. We knew that we must soon overtake two detachments of barges; but we sailed one day, two days, and there was no trace of them. My friend Maróvsky lost both sleep and appetite, and looked as if he had just had a serious illness. He sat whole days on the deck, motionless, murmuring: 'All is lost, all is lost!' The villages are few and rare in this part of the Amúr, and nobody could give us any information. A new storm came on, and when we reached at last a village, we learned that no barges had passed by it, and that quantities of wreck had been seen floating down the river during the previous day. It was evident that at least forty barges, which carried a cargo of about 2,000 tons, must have perished. It meant a certain famine next spring on the lower Amúr if no supplies were brought in time. We were late in the season, navigation would soon be closed, and there was no telegraph yet along the river.

We held a council and decided that Maróvsky should sail as quickly as possible to the mouth of the Amúr. Some purchases of grain might perhaps be made in Japan before the close of the navigation. Meanwhile I was to go with all possible speed up the river, to determine the losses, and do my best to cover

the two thousand miles of the Amúr and the Shílka—
in boats, on horseback, or on board steamer if I met
one. The sooner I could warn the Chitá authorities,
and despatch any amount of provisions available, the
better it would be. Perhaps part of them would
reach this same autumn the upper Amúr, whence it
would be easier to ship them in the early spring to the
lowlands. Even if a few weeks or only days could be
won, it might make an immense difference in case of a
famine.

I began my two thousand miles' journey in a
rowing boat, changing rowers each twenty miles or so,
at each village. It was very slow progress, but there
might be no steamer coming up the river for a fortnight, and in the meantime I could reach the spots
where the barges were wrecked and see if any of the
provisions had been saved. Then, at the mouth of the
Usurí (Khabaróvsk) I might find a steamer. The
boats which I took in the villages were miserable, and
the weather very stormy. We kept evidently along
the shore, but we had to cross some branches of the
Amúr of great width, and the waves, driven by the
high wind, threatened continually to swamp our little
craft. One day we had to cross a branch of the Amúr
nearly half a mile wide. Chopped waves rose like
mountains as they rolled up that branch. My rowers,
two peasants, were seized with terror; their faces
were white as paper; their blue lips trembled, they
murmured prayers. Only a boy of fifteen, who held
the rudder, calmly kept a watchful eye upon the waves.
He glided between them as they seemed to sink
around us for a moment; but when he saw them

rising to a menacing height in front of us he gave a
slight turn to the boat and steadied it across the waves.
The boat shipped water from each wave, and I threw it
out with an old ladle, noting at times that it accumu-
lated more rapidly than I could get rid of it. There
was a moment when the boat shipped two such big
waves that, on a sign given to me by one of the
trembling rowers, I unfastened the heavy sackful of
copper and silver that I carried across my shoulder. . .
For several days in succession we had such crossings.
I never forced the men to cross, but they themselves,
knowing why I had to hurry, would decide at a given
moment that an attempt must be made. 'There are
not seven deaths in one's life, and one cannot be
avoided,' they would say, and, signing themselves with
the cross, would seize the oars and pull over.

I soon reached the places where the main destruction of our barges took place. Forty-four barges had
been destroyed, by the storm. Unloading had been
impossible, and very little of the cargo had been saved.
Two thousand tons of flour had perished in the waves.
With this message I continued my journey.

A few days later a steamer slowly creeping up
the river overtook me, and when I boarded her the
passengers told me that the captain had drunk so
much that he was seized with delirium and jumped
overboard. He was saved, though, and was now lying
ill in his cabin. They asked me to take the command
of the steamer, and I had to accept it; but soon I
realized, to my great astonishment, that everything went
on by itself in such an excellent routine way that,
though I paraded all day on the bridge, I had almost

nothing to do. Apart from a few minutes of real responsibility when the steamer had to be brought to the landing-places, where we took wood for fuel, and saying a few words now and then for encouraging the stokers to start as soon as dawn permitted us faintly to distinguish the outlines of the shores, everything went on by itself, requiring but little interference of mine. A pilot who would have been able to interpret the map would have managed as well.

Travelling by steamer and a great deal on horseback I reached at last Transbaikália. The idea of a famine that might break out next spring on the lower Amúr oppressed me all the time. I found that the small steamer on board of which I was did not progress up the swift Shílka rapidly enough, and in order to gain some twenty hours, or even less, I abandoned it and rode with a Cossack a couple of hundred miles up the Argúñ, along one of the wildest mountain tracks in Siberia, stopping to light our camp fire only after midnight would have overtaken us in the woods. Even the ten or twenty hours that I might gain by this exertion had not to be despised, because every day brought us nearer to the close of navigation : at nights, ice was already forming on the river. At last I met the Governor of Transbaikália, and my friend, Colonel Pedashénko, on the Shílka, at the convict settlement of Kará, and the latter took in hand the care of shipping immediately all available provisions. As to me, I left immediately to report all about the matter at Irkútsk.

People at Irkútsk wondered that I had managed to make this long journey so rapidly, but I was quite worn out. However, youth quickly recovers its strength,-

and I recovered mine by sleeping for some time such a number of hours every day that I should be ashamed to say how many.

'Have you taken some rest?' the Governor-General asked me a week or so after my arrival. 'Could you start to-morrow for St. Petersburg, as a courier, to report there yourself upon the loss of the barges?'

It meant to cover in twenty days—not one day more—another distance of 3,200 miles between Irkútsk and Níjni-Nóvgorod, where I could take the railway to St. Petersburg; to gallop day and night in post-carts which had to be changed at every station, because no carriage would stand such a journey full speed over the ruts of the roads frozen at the end of the autumn. But to see my brother Alexander was too great an attraction for me not to accept the offer, and I started the next night. When I reached the lowlands of West Siberia and the Urals the journey really became a torture. There were days when the wheels of the carts would be broken over the frozen ruts at every successive station. The rivers were freezing, and I had to cross the Ob in a boat amidst the floating ice, which menaced at every moment to crush our small craft. When I reached the Tom river, on which the ice had only stopped floating during the preceding night, the peasants refused for some time to take me over, asking me to give them 'a receipt.'

'What sort of receipt do you want?'

'Well, you write on a paper: "I, undersigned, hereby testify that I was drowned by the will of God and by no fault of the peasants," and you give us that paper.'

Q 2

'With pleasure, on the other shore.'

At last they took me over. A boy—a brave, bright
boy whom I had selected in the crowd—opened the
procession, testing the strength of the ice with a pole ;
I followed him, carrying my despatch-box on my
shoulders, and we two were attached to long reins which
five peasants held, following us at a distance—one of
them carrying a bundle of straw, to be thrown on the
ice if it should not seem strong enough.

At last I reached Moscow, where my brother met
me at the station, and we proceeded at once to St.
Petersburg.

Youth is a grand thing. After such a journey,
which lasted twenty-four days and nights, when I came,
early in the morning, to St. Petersburg, I went the
same day to deliver my despatches, and did not fail also
to call upon an aunt—or, rather, upon a cousin—
who resided at St. Petersburg. She was radiant.
'We have a dancing party to-night. Will you
come?' she said. Of course I would! And not only
come, but dance until an early hour of the morning.

When I came to St. Petersburg and saw the
authorities, I understood why I had been sent to
make the report. Nobody would believe the possibility
of such a destruction of the barges. 'Have you been
on the spot? Did you see the destruction with
your own eyes? Are you perfectly sure that
"they" have not simply stolen the provisions and
shown you the wreck of some barges?' Such were
the questions I had to answer.

The high functionaries who stood at the head of

Siberian affairs at St. Petersburg were simply charming in their innocent ignorance of Siberia. '*Mais, mon cher,*' one of them said to me—he always spoke French—'how *is* it possible that forty barges should be destroyed on the Nevá without anyone rushing to help save them?' 'The Nevá,' I exclaimed; 'put three, four Nevás side by side, and you will have the lower Amúr!'

'Is it really as big as that?' And two minutes later he was chatting, in excellent French, about all sorts of things. 'When did you last see Schwartz, the painter? Is not his " John the Terrible " a wonderful picture? Do you know for what reason Kúkel was going to be arrested? Do you know that Cherny-shévsky is arrested? He is now in the fortress.'

'What for? What has he done?' I asked.

'Nothing particular; nothing! But, *mon cher*, you know, State considerations! Such a clever man, awfully clever! And such an influence he has upon the youth. You understand that a Government cannot tolerate that : that's impossible! *intolérable, mon cher, dans un État bien ordonné!*'

Count Ignátieff made no such questions; he knew the Amúr very well, and he knew St. Petersburg too. Amidst all sorts of jokes, and witty remarks about Siberia which he made with an astounding vivacity, he dropped to me : 'It is a very lucky thing that you were there on the spot, and saw the wrecks. And " they " were clever to send you with the report! Well done! At first, nobody wanted to believe about the barges. Some new swindling, it was thought. But now people say that you were well known as a page, and you have only been a few months in Siberia ; so you would not shelter the people there if it were swindling. They trust in you.'

The Minister of War, Dmítri Milútin, was the only man in the high administration of St. Petersburg who took the matter seriously. He asked me many questions : all to the point. He mastered the subject at once, and all our conversation was in short sentences, without hurry, but without any waste of words. 'The coast settlements to be supplied from the sea, you mean ? The remainder only from Chitá? Quite right. But if a storm happens next year, will there be the same destruction once more?' 'No, if there are two small tugs to convoy the barges.' 'Will it do?' 'Yes, with one tug the loss would not have been half so heavy.' 'Very probably. Write to me, please; state all you have said, quite plainly ; no formalities.'

V

I DID not stay long at St. Petersburg, and returned to Irkútsk the same winter. My brother was going to join me there in a few months ; he was accepted as an officer of the Irkútsk Cossacks.

Travelling across Siberia in the winter is supposed to be a terrible experience; but, all things considered, it is on the whole more comfortable than at any other season of the year. The snow-covered roads are excellent, and, although the cold is fearful, one can stand it well enough. Lying full length in the sledge—as everyone does in Siberia—wrapped in fur blankets, fur inside and fur outside, one does not suffer much from the cold, even when the temperature is forty or sixty Fahrenheit degrees below zero. Travelling in courier fashion—that is, rapidly changing horses at each station and stopping only once a day for one hour to take a meal—I reached Irkútsk nineteen days after I had left St. Petersburg. Two hundred miles a day is the normal speed in such cases, and I remember having covered the last 660 miles before Irkútsk in seventy hours. The frost was not severe then, the roads were in an excellent condition, the drivers were kept in good spirits by a free allowance of silver coins, and the team of three small and light horses seemed to enjoy running swiftly across hill and vale, and across rivers frozen as hard as steel, amidst forests glistening in their silver attire in the rays of the sun.

I was now nominated attaché to the Governor-General of East Siberia for Cossack affairs, and had to reside at Irkútsk; but there was nothing particular to do. To let everything go on, according to the established routine, with no more reference to changes, such was the watchword that came now from St. Petersburg. I therefore gladly accepted the proposal to undertake geographical exploration in Manchuria.

If one casts a glance on a map of Asia one sees that the Russian frontier, which runs in Siberia, broadly speaking, along the fiftieth degree of latitude, suddenly bends in Transbaikália to the north. It follows for three hundred miles the Argúñ river; then, on reaching the Amúr, it turns south-eastwards—the town of

Blagovéschensk, which was the capital of the Amúr land, being situated again in about the same latitude of fifty degrees. Between the south-eastern corner of Transbaikália (New Tsurukháitu) and Blagovéschensk on the Amúr, the distance west to east is only five hundred miles; but along the Argún and the Amúr it is over a thousand miles, and moreover communication along the Argún, which is not navigable, is extremely difficult. In its lower parts there is nothing but a most wild mountain track.

Transbaikália is very rich in cattle, and the Cossacks who occupy its south-eastern corner, and are wealthy cattle-breeders, wanted to establish a direct communication with the middle Amúr, which would be a good market for their cattle. They used to trade with the Mongols, and they had heard from them that it would not be difficult to reach the Amúr, travelling eastwards across the Great Khingán. Going straight towards the east, they were told, one would fall in with an old Chinese route which crosses the Khingán and leads to the Manchurian town of Merghén (on the Nónni river, a tributary to the Sungarí), whence an excellent road leads to the middle Amúr.

I was offered the leadership of a trading caravan which the Cossacks intended to organize in order to find that route, and I accepted it with enthusiasm. No European had ever visited that region, and a Russian topographer who went that way a few years before was killed. Only two Jesuits, in the time of the emperor Kan-si, had penetrated from the south as far as Merghén, and had determined its latitude. All the immense region to the north of it, five hundred miles wide and five hundred miles deep, was totally, absolutely unknown. I consulted all the available sources about this region. Nobody, not even the Chinese geographers, knew anything about it. Besides, the very fact of connecting the middle Amúr with Transbaikália had its importance ; Tsurukháitu is now going to be the head of the Trans-Manchuria railway. We were thus the pioneers of that great enterprise.

There was, however, one difficulty. The treaty with China granted to the Russians free trade with the 'Empire of China and Mongolia.' Manchuria was not mentioned in it, and could as well be excluded as included in the treaty. The Chinese frontier authorities interpreted it one way, and the Russians the other way. Moreover, only trade being mentioned, an officer would not be allowed to enter Manchuria: I had thus to go as a trader, and accordingly I bought at Irkútsk various goods, and went disguised as a merchant. The Governor-General delivered me a passport, 'To the Irkútsk second guild merchant Petr Alexéiev and his companions,' and he warned me that if the Chinese authorities arrested me and took me to Pekin, and thence across the Góbi to the Russian frontier—in a cage on a camel's back was their way of conveying prisoners across Mongolia—I must not betray him by naming myself. I accepted, of course, all the conditions, the temptation to visit a country which no European had ever seen being too great for an explorer.

It would not have been easy to conceal my identity while I was in Transbaikália. The Cossacks are an extremely inquisitive sort of people—real

Mongols—and as soon as a stranger comes to one of their villages, while treating him with the greatest hospitality, the master of the house submits the new-comer to a formal interrogatory.

'A tedious journey, I suppose,' he begins; 'a long way from Chitá, is it not? And then, perhaps, longer still for one who comes from some place beyond Chitá? Maybe from Irkútsk? Trading there, I believe? Many tradesmen come this way. You are going also to Nerchínsk, I should say?— Yes, people are often married at your age; and you, too, must have left a family, I suppose? Many children? Not all boys, I should say?' And so on for quite half an hour.

The local commander of the Cossacks, Captain Buxhövden, knew his people, and consequently we had taken our precautions. At Chitá and at Irkútsk we often had had amateur theatricals, playing in preference dramas of Ostróvsky, in which the scene of action is nearly always amongst the merchant classes. I played several times in different dramas, and found such great pleasure in acting that I even wrote on one occasion to my brother an enthusiastic letter confessing to him my passionate desire to abandon my military career and to go on the stage. I played mostly young merchants, and had so well got hold of their ways of talking and gesticulating, and tea-drinking from the saucer—I knew these ways since my Nikólskoye experiences—that now I had a good opportunity to act it all out in reality for useful purposes.

'Take your seat, Petr Alexéievich,' Captain Buxhövden would say to me, when the boiling tea-urn, throwing out clouds of steam, was placed on the table.

'Thank you; we may stay here,' I would reply, sitting on the edge of a chair at a distance, and beginning to drink my tea in true Moscow-merchant fashion. Buxhövden meanwhile nearly exploded with laughter as I blew upon my saucer with staring eyes, and bit off in a special way microscopic particles from a small lump of sugar which was to serve for half a dozen cups.

. We knew that the Cossacks would soon make out the truth about me, but the important thing was to win a few days only, and to cross the frontier while my identity was not yet discovered. I must have played my part pretty well, as the Cossacks treated me as a small merchant. In one village an old woman beckoned me in the passage and asked me: 'Are there more people coming behind you on the road, my dear?' 'None, grandmother, that we heard of.' 'They said a prince, Rapótsky, was going to come. Is he coming?'

'Oh, I see. You are right, grandmother. His Highness intended to go, too, from Irkútsk. But how can he? Such a journey! Not suitable for them. So they remained where they were.'

'Of course, how can he?'

In short, we crossed the frontier unmolested. We were eleven Cossacks, one Tungus, and myself, all on horseback. We had with us about forty horses for sale and two carts, one of which, two-wheeled, belonged to me, and contained the cloth, the velveteen, the gold braid, and so on, which I had taken in my capacity of merchant. I attended to it and to my horses entirely myself, while we chose one of the Cossacks to be the ' elder ' of our caravan. He had to manage all the diplomatic talk with the Chinese authorities. All Cossacks spoke Mongolian, and the Tungus understood Manchurian. The Cossacks of the caravan knew, of course, who I was—one of them knew me at Irkútsk—but they never betrayed that knowledge, understanding that the success of the expedition depended upon it. I wore a long blue cotton dress, like the others, and the Chinese paid no attention to me, so that I could make, unnoticed by them, the compass survey of the route. The first day only, when all sorts of Chinese soldiers hung about us in the hope of getting a glass of whisky, I had often to cast only a furtive glance at my compass and to inscribe the bearings and the distances in my pocket, without taking my paper out. We had with us no arms whatever. Only our Tungus, who was going to marry, had taken his matchlock gun and used it to hunt for fallow deer, bringing us meat for supper, and making a provision of furs with which to pay for his future wife.

When there was no more whisky to be obtained from us the Chinese soldiers left us alone. So we went straight eastwards, finding our way as best we could across hill and dale, and after a four or five days' march we really fell in with the Chinese track which had to take us across the Khingán to Merghén.

To our astonishment we discovered that the crossing of the great ridge, which looked so black and terrible on the maps, was most easy. We overtook on the road an old Chinese functionary, miserably wretched, who travelled in the same direction in a two-wheeled cart. For the last two days the road was going up hill, and the country bore testimony to its high altitude. The ground became marshy, and the road was muddy; the grass was very poor, and the trees grew thin, undeveloped, often crippled and covered with lichens. Mountains devoid of forests rose right and left, and we thought already of the difficulties we should experience in crossing the ridge, when we saw the old Chinese functionary alighting from his cart before an *obó*—that is, before a heap made of stones and branches of trees to which bundles of horsehair and small rags had been attached. He drew several hairs out of the mane of his horse, and attached them to the branches.

'What is that?' we asked.

'The *obó*—the waters before us flow now to the Amúr.'

'Is that all of the Khingán?'

'Yes! No mountains more to cross as far as the Amúr: only hills!'

Quite a commotion spread in our caravan. 'The rivers flow to the Amúr, the Amúr!' shouted the Cossacks to each other. All their lives they had heard the old Cossacks talking about the great river where the vine grows wild, where the prairies extend for hundreds of miles and could give wealth to millions of men; then, after the Amúr was annexed to Russia, they heard of the long journey to it, the difficulties of the first settlers, and the prosperity of their relatives settled on the upper Amúr; and now we had found the short way to it! We had before us a steep

slope upon which the road went downwards in zig-zags
leading to a small river, which pierced its way through
a chopped sea of mountains, and led to the Amúr.   No
more obstacles lay between us and the great river.   A
traveller will imagine my delight at this unexpected geographical discovery.   As to the Cossacks, they hastened
to dismount and to attach in their turn bundles of hair
taken from their horses to the branches thrown on the
obó.   The Siberians altogether have a sort of awe for
the gods of the heathen.   They don't think much of
them, but these gods, they say, are wickèd creatures,
bent on mischief, and it is never good to be on bad
terms with them.   It is far better to bribe them with
small tokens of respect.

'Look, here is a strange tree : it must be an oak,'
they exclaimed, as we went down the steep slope.   The
oak does not grow, indeed, in Siberia.   None is found
until the eastern slope of the high plateau has been
reached.   'Look, nut trees!' they exclaimed next.
'And what tree is that?' they said, seeing a lime tree,
or some other tree which does not grow in Russia either,
but which I knew as part of the Manchurian flora.
The northerners, who for centuries had dreamed of
warmer lands, and now saw them, were in delight.
Lying on the ground covered with rich grass, they
caressed it with their eyes—they would have kissed it.
Now they burned with the desire to reach the Amúr as
soon as possible.   When, a fortnight later, we stopped
at our last camp fire within twenty miles from the
river, they grew impatient like children.   They began
to saddle their horses shortly after midnight, and
hurried me to start long before daybreak ; and when at

last we caught from an eminence a sight of the
mighty stream, the eyes of these unimpressionable
Siberians, generally devoid of poetical feeling, gleamed
with poetical ardour as they looked upon the blue
waters of the majestic Amúr.   It was evident that,
sooner or later—with or without the support, or even
against the wish, of the Russian Government—both
banks of this river, a desert now but rich in possibilities,
as well as the immense unpopulated stretches of North
Manchuria, would be invaded by Russian settlers, just
as the shores of the Mississippi were colonized by the
Canadian *voyageurs.*

In the meantime the old half-blind Chinese
functionary with whom we had crossed the Khingán,
having donned his blue coat and official hat with a
glass button on its top, declared to us next morning
that he would not let us go further.   Our 'elder' had
received him and his clerk in our tent, and the old
man, repeating what the clerk whispered to him, raised
all sorts of objections to our further progress.   He
wanted us to camp on the spot while he would send
our pass to Pekin to get orders, which we absolutely
refused to do.   Then he sought to quarrel with our
passport.

'What sort of a passport is that?' he said, looking
with disdain into our pass, which was written in a few
lines on a plain sheet of foolscap paper, in Russian and
Mongolian, and had a simple sealing-wax seal.   'You
may have written it yourselves and sealed it with a
copper,' he remarked.   'Look at my pass: this is
worth something,' and he unrolled before us a sheet of
paper, two feet long, covered with Chinese characters.

I sat quietly aside during this conference, packing something in my box, when a sheet of the ' Moscow Gazette' fell under my hand.   The Gazette, being the property of the Moscow University, had an eagle printed on its title-heading.   ' Show him this,' I said to our elder.   He unfolded the large sheet of print and pointed out the eagle.   ' That pass was to show to you,' our elder said, ' but this is what we have for ourselves.'

' Why, is it all written about you ? ' the old man asked with terror.

' All about us,' our elder replied, without even a twinkle in his eyes.

The old man—a true functionary—looked quite dumbfounded at seeing such a profusion of writing. He examined every one of us, nodding with his head. But the clerk was still whispering something to his chief, who finally declared that he would not let us continue the journey.

' Enough of talking,' I said to the elder ; ' give the order to saddle the horses.'   The Cossacks were of the same opinion, and in no time our caravan started, bidding good-bye to the old functionary and promising him to report that short of resorting to violence—which he was not able to do—he had done all in his power to prevent us from entering Manchuria, and that it was our fault if we went nevertheless.

A few days later we were at Merghén, where we traded a little, and soon reached the Chinese town of Aigún, on the right bank of the Amúr, and the Russian town of Blagovéschensk, on the left bank.   We had discovered the direct route and many interesting things besides : the border-ridge character of the Great

Khinghán, the ease with which it can be crossed, the
tertiary volcanoes of the Uyún Kholdontsí region,
which had so long been a puzzle in geographical
literature, and so on.   I cannot say that I was a sharp
tradesman, for at Merghén I persisted (in broken
Chinese) in asking thirty-five roubles for a watch when
the Chinese buyer had already offered me forty-five;
but the Cossacks traded all right.   They sold very
well all their horses, and when my horses, my goods,
and the rest were sold by the Cossacks it appeared that
the expedition had cost the government the modest
sum of twenty-two roubles—a little over two pounds.

<hr />

VI

ALL this summer I travelled on the Amúr.   I went as
far as its mouth, or rather its estuary—Nikoláevsk—to
join the Governor-General, whom I accompanied in a
steamer up the Usurí; and after that, in the autumn, I
made a still more interesting journey up the Sungarí,
to the very heart of Manchuria, as far as Ghirín (or
Kirín, according to the southern pronunciation).

Many rivers in Asia are formed by the junction of two
equally important streams, so that it is difficult for the
geographer to say which of the two is the main one and
which is a tributary.   The Ingodá and the Onón join
to make the Shílka; the Shílka and the Argúñ join to
make the Amúr; and the Amúr joins the Sungarí to
form that mighty stream which flows north-eastwards

and enters the Pacific in the inhospitable latitudes of the Tartar Strait.

Up to the year 1864 the great river of Manchúria remained very little known. All information about it dated from the times of the Jesuits, and that was scanty. Now that a revival in the exploration of Mongolia and Manchuria was going to take place, and the fear of China which had hitherto been entertained in Russia appeared to be exaggerated, all of us younger people pressed upon the Governor-General the necessity of exploring the Sungarí. To have next door to the Amúr an immense region almost as little known as an African desert seemed to us provoking. Quite unexpectedly, General Korsákoff decided that same autumn to send a steamer up the Sungarí, under the pretext of carrying some message of friendship to the Governor-General of the Ghirín province. A Russian consul from Urgá had to take the message. A doctor, an astronomer, two topographers, and myself, all placed under the command of a Colonel Chernyáeff, had to take part in the expedition on board a tiny steamer, *Usuri*, which had in tow a barge with coal. Twenty-five soldiers, whose rifles were carefully concealed in the coal, went with us on the barge.

All was organized very hurriedly, and there was no accommodation on the small steamer to receive such a numerous company ; but we were all full of enthusiasm, and huddled as best we could in the tiny cabins. One of us had to sleep on a table, and when we started we found that there were even no knives and forks for all of us—not to speak of other necessaries. One of us resorted to his penknife at dinner time, and my Chinese

knife with two ivory sticks was a welcome addition to
our equipment.

It was not an easy task to go up the Sungarí. The
great river, in its lower parts, where it flows through
the same lowlands as the Amúr, is very shallow, and,
although our steamer had only three feet draught, we
often could not find a channel deep enough to pass
through. There were days when we advanced but some
forty miles, and scraped many times the sandy bottom
of the river with our keel ; over and over again a rowing
boat was sent out to find the necessary depth. But our
young captain had made up his mind that he would
reach Ghirín this autumn, and we progressed every day.
As we advanced higher and higher up we found the river
more and more beautiful, and more and more easy for
navigation ; and when we had passed the sandy deserts
at its junction with its sister-river, the Nónni, navigation
became easy and pleasant. In a few weeks we reached
the capital óf this province of Manchuria. An excellent map of the river was made by the topographers.

There was no time, unfortunately, to spare, and so
we very seldom landed in any village or town. The
villages are few and rare along the banks of the river,
and in its lower parts we found only lowlands, which
are inundated every year. Higher up we sailed for a
hundred miles amidst sand dunes. It was only when
we reached the upper Sungarí and began to approach
Ghirín that we found a dense population.

If our aim had been to establish friendly relations
with Manchuria—and not simply to learn what the
Sungarí is—our expedition ought to have been considered a dead failure. The Manchurian authorities had

it fresh in their memories how, eight years before, the 'visit' of Muravióff ended in the annexation of the Amúr and the Usurí, and they could not but look with suspicion on these new and uncalled-for visitors. The twenty-five rifles concealed in the coal, which had been duly reported to the Chinese authorities before we left, still more provoked their suspicions; and when our steamer cast her anchor in front of the populous city of Ghirín we found all its merchants armed with rusty swords, unearthed from some old arsenal. We were not prevented, however, from walking in the streets, but all shops were closed as soon as we landed and the merchants were not allowed to sell anything. Some provisions were sent on board the steamer—as a gift, but no money was taken in return.

The autumn was rapidly coming to its end, the frosts began already, and we had to hurry back, as we could not winter on the Sungarí. In short, we saw Ghirín, but spoke to none but the couple of interpreters who came every morning on board our steamer. Our aim, however, was fulfilled. We had ascertained that the river is navigable, and a detailed map of it was made, from its mouth to Ghirín, with the aid of which we were able to steam on our return journey at full speed without any accident. Our steamer only once touched the ground. But the Ghirín authorities, desirous above all that we should not be compelled to winter on the river, sent us two hundred Chinese, who aided us in getting off the sands. When I jumped into the water and, also taking a stick, began to sing our river song, 'Dubínushka,' which helps all present to give a sudden push at the same moment, the Chinese enjoyed immensely the fun of it, and after several such pushes the steamer was soon afloat. The most cordial relations were established after this little adventure between ourselves and the Chinese —I mean, of course, the people, who seemed to dislike very much their arrogant Manchurian officials.

We called at several Chinese villages peopled with exiles from the celestial empire, and we were received in the most cordial way. One evening especially impressed itself on my memory. We came to a small, picturesque village as night was already falling. Some of us landed, and I went alone through the village. A thick crowd of a hundred Chinese soon surrounded me, and although I knew not a word of their tongue, and they knew no more of mine, we chatted in the most amicable way by mimicry and we understood each other. To pat one on the shoulders in sign of friendship is decidedly international language. To offer each other tobacco and to be offered a light is again an international expression of friendship. One thing interested them—why had I, though young, a beard? They wear none before they are sixty. And when I told them by signs that in case I should have nothing to eat I might eat it—the joke was transmitted from one to the other through the whole crowd. They roared with laughter, and began to pat me even more caressingly on the shoulders; they took me about, showing me their houses, everyone offered me his pipe, and the whole crowd accompanied me as a friend to the steamer. I must say that there was not one single *boshkó* (policeman) in that village. In other villages our soldiers and the young officers always made friends with the Chinese, but as soon as a *boshkó* appeared all was spoiled. In return, one must have seen what 'faces' they used to make at the *boshkó* behind his back ! They evidently hated these representatives of authority.

Our expedition has since been forgotten. The astronomer, Th. Usóltzeff, and I published reports about it in the 'Memoirs' of the Siberian Geographical Society ; but a few years later a great conflagration at Irkútsk destroyed all the copies left of the Memoirs as well as the original map of the Sungarí, and it was only last year, when the Trans-Manchurian railway began to be built, that Russian geographers unearthed our reports, and found that the great river had been explored five-and-thirty years ago.

VII

As there was nothing more to be done in the direction of reform, I tried to do what seemed to be possible under the existing circumstances—only to become convinced of the absolute uselessness of such efforts. In my new capacity of attaché to the Governor-General for Cossack affairs, I made, for instance, a most thorough investigation of the economical condition of the Usurí Cossacks, whose crops used to be lost every year, so that the government had every winter to feed them in order to save them from famine. When I returned from the Usurí with my report, I received congratulations on all sides, I was promoted, I got special rewards. All the measures I recommended were accepted, and special grants of money were given for aiding the emigration of some and for supplying cattle to others, as I had suggested. But the practical realization of the measures went into the hands of some old drunkard, who would squander the money and pitilessly flog the unfortunate Cossacks for the purpose of converting them into good agriculturalists. And thus it went on in all directions, beginning with the winter palace at St. Petersburg and ending with the Usurí and Kamchátka.

The higher administration of Siberia was influenced by excellent intentions, and I can only repeat that, everything considered, it was far better, far more enlightened, and far more interested in the welfare of the people than the administration of any other province of Russia. But it was an administration—a branch of the tree which had its roots at St. Petersburg—and that was enough to paralyse all its excellent intentions, enough to make it interfere with and kill all the beginnings of local life and progress. Whatever was started for the good of the country by local men was looked at with distrust, and was immediately paralysed by hosts of difficulties which came, not so much from the bad intentions of the administrators, but simply from the fact that these officials belonged to a pyramidal, centralised administration. The very fact of their belonging to a government which radiated from a distant capital caused them to look upon everything from the point of view of functionaries of the government, who think first of all about what their superiors will say, and how this or that will appear in the administrative machinery. The interests of the country are a secondary matter.

Gradually I turned my energy more and more toward scientific exploration. In 1865 I explored the western Sayáns, where I caught a new glimpse of the structure of the Siberian highlands and came upon another important volcanic region on the Chinese frontier ; and finally, the year following, I undertook a long journey to discover a direct communication between the gold mines of the Yakútsk province (on the Vitím and the Olókma) and Transbaikália. For many years the members of the Siberian expedition (1860–1864) had tried to find such a passage, and had endeavoured to cross the series of very wild, stony parallel ridges which separate these mines from the plains of Transbaikália ; but when, coming from the south, they reached that gloomy mountain region, and saw before them the dreary mountains spreading for hundreds of miles northward, all of these explorers, save one who was killed by natives, returned southward. It was evident that in order to be successful the expedition had to move from the north to the south—from the dreary unknown wilderness to the warmer and populated regions. It so happened, also, that while I was preparing for the expedition I was shown a map which a Tungus had traced with his knife on a piece of bark. This little map—a splendid specimen, by the way, of the usefulness of the geometrical sense in the lowest stages of civilization, and one which would consequently interest A. R. Wallace—so struck me by its seeming truth to nature that I fully trusted to it, and began my journey from the north, following the indications of the map.

In company with a young and promising naturalist, Polakóff, and a topographer, we went first down the Léna to the northern gold mines. There we equipped the expedition, taking provisions for three months, and started southward. An old Yakút hunter, who twenty years before had once followed the passage indicated in the Tungus map, undertook to act for us as a guide and to cross the mountain region—250 miles wide—following the river-valleys and gorges indicated by the Tungus with his knife on the birch-bark map. He really accomplished that astounding feat, although there was no track of any sort to follow, and all the valleys that one saw from the top of a mountain pass, all equally covered with wood, seemed to be absolutely alike to the unpractised eye. This time the passage was found. For three months we wandered in the almost totally uninhabited mountain deserts and over the marshy plateau, till at last we reached our destination, Chitá. I am told that this passage is now of value for bringing cattle from the south to the gold mines; as for me, the journey helped me immensely afterwards in finding the key to the structure of the mountains and plateaus of Siberia—but I am not writing a book of travel, and must stop.

The years that I spent in Siberia taught me many lessons which I could hardly have learned elsewhere. I soon realized the absolute impossibility of doing anything really useful for the masses of the people by means of the administrative machinery. With this

illusion I parted for ever.   Then I began to understand
not only men and human character, but also the inner
springs of the life of human society.   The constructive
work of the unknown masses, which so seldom finds
any mention in books, and the importance of that
constructive work in the growth of forms of society,
appeared before my eyes in a clear light.   To witness, for instance, the ways in which the communities of Dukhobórtsy (brothers of those who are now
settling in Canada, and who found such a hearty support
in England and the United States) migrated to the Amúr
region ; to see the immense advantages which they got
from their semi-communistic brotherly organization ;
and to realize what a success their colonization
was, amidst all the failures of State colonization, was
learning something which cannot be learned from
books.   Again, to live with natives, to see at work
the complex forms of social organization which they
have elaborated far away from the influence of any
civilization, was, as it were, to store up floods of light
which illuminated my subsequent reading.   The part
which the unknown masses play in the accomplishment
of all important historical events, and even in war,
became evident to me from direct observation, and I
came to hold ideas similar to those which Tolstoy
expresses concerning the leaders and the masses in his
monumental work, ' War and Peace.'

Having been brought up in a serf-owner's family, I
entered active life, like all young men of my time, with
a great deal of confidence in the necessity of commanding, ordering, scolding, punishing, and the like.   But
when, at an early stage, I had to manage serious enter-

prises and to deal with men, and when each mistake would lead at once to heavy consequences, I began to appreciate the difference between acting on the principle of command and discipline, and acting on the principle of common understanding. The former works admirably in a military parade, but it is worth nothing where real life is concerned and the aim can be achieved only through the severe effort of many converging wills. Although I did not then formulate my observations in terms borrowed from party struggles, I may say now that I lost in Siberia whatever faith in State discipline I had cherished before. I was prepared to become an anarchist.

From the age of nineteen to twenty-five I had to work out important schemes of reform, to deal with hundreds of men on the Amúr, to prepare and to make risky expeditions with ridiculously small means, and so on ; and if all these things ended more or less successfully, I account for it only by the fact that I soon understood that in serious work commanding and discipline are of little avail. Men of initiative are required everywhere ; but once the impulse has been given, the enterprise must be conducted, especially in Russia, not in military fashion, but in a sort of communal way, by means of common understanding. I wish that all framers of plans of State discipline could pass through the school of real life before they begin to frame their State Utopias : we should then hear far less than at present of schemes of military and pyramidal organization of society.

With all that, life in Siberia became less and less attractive for me, although my brother Alexander had joined me in 1864 at Irkútsk, where he commanded a

squadron of Cossacks.   We were happy to be together ;
we read a great deal and discussed all the philosophical,
scientific, and sociological questions of the day ; but we
both longed after intellectual life, and there was none
in Siberia.   The occasional passage through Irkútsk of
Raphael Pumpelly or of Adolph Bastian—the only two
men of science who visited our capital during my stay
there—was   quite   an   event   for   both   of   us.   The
scientific and especially the political life of Western
Europe,   of   which   we   heard   through   the   papers,
attracted us, and the return to Russia was the subject
to which we continually came back in our conversations.   Finally, the insurrection of the Polish exiles in
1866 opened our eyes to the false position we both
occupied as officers of the Russian army.

VIII

I was far away in the Vitím mountains when some
Polish exiles, who were employed in piercing a new road
in the cliffs round Lake Baikál, made a desperate attempt
to break their chains and to force their way to China
across Mongolia.   Troops were sent out against them,
and a Russian officer was killed by the insurgents.
I heard of it on my return to Irkútsk, where some fifty
Poles were to be tried by a court-martial.   The sittings
of courts-martial being open in Russia, I followed this,
taking detailed notes of the proceedings, which I sent
to a St. Petersburg paper, and which were published

in full, to the great dissatisfaction of the Governor-General.

Eleven thousand Poles, men and women, had been transported to East Siberia in consequence of the insurrection of 1863. They were chiefly students, artists, ex-officers, nobles, and especially skilled artisans from the intelligent and highly developed working-men's population of Warsaw and other towns. A great number of them were kept in hard labour, while the remainder were settled all over the country in villages where they could find no work whatever and lived in a state of semi-starvation. Those who were condemned to hard labour worked either at Chitá, building the barges for the Amúr—these were the happiest—or in iron works of the Crown, or in salt works. I saw some of the latter, on the Léna, standing half-naked in a shanty, round an immense cauldron filled with salt-brine, and mixing the thick, boiling brine with long shovels, in an infernal temperature, while the gates of the shanty were wide open to make a strong current of glacial air. After two years of such work these martyrs were sure to die from consumption.

Lately, a considerable number of Polish exiles were employed as navvies building a road along the southern coast of Lake Baikál. This narrow Alpine lake, four hundred miles long, surrounded by beautiful mountains rising three to five thousand feet above its level, cuts off Transbaikália and the Amúr from Irkútsk. In winter it may be crossed over the ice and in summer there are steamers, but for six weeks in the spring and another six weeks in the autumn the only means to reach Chitá and Kyákhta (for Pekin) from Irkútsk was to travel on horseback a long circuitous route, across mountains 7,000 to 8,000 feet in altitude. I once travelled along this track, greatly enjoying the scenery of the mountains, which were snow-clad in May, but otherwise the journey was really awful. To climb eight miles only, to the top of the main pass, Khamár-dabán, it took me the whole day from three in the morning till eight at night. Our horses continually fell through the thawing snow, plunging with the rider many times a day into icy water which flowed underneath the snow-crust. It was decided accordingly to build a permanent road along the southern coast of the lake, blowing up a passage in the steep, almost vertical cliffs which rise along the shore, and spanning with bridges a hundred wild torrents which furiously rush from the mountains into the lake. Polish exiles were employed at this hard work.

Several batches of Russian political exiles had been sent during the last century to Siberia, but, with the submissiveness to fate which is characteristic of the Russians, they never revolted ; they allowed themselves to be killed inch by inch, without ever attempting to free themselves. The Poles, on the contrary—this must be said to their honour—were never so submissive as that, and this time they broke into open revolt. They evidently had no chance of success—they revolted nevertheless. They had before them the great lake, and behind them a girdle of absolutely impracticable mountains, beyond which begin the wildernesses of North Mongolia ; but they nevertheless conceived the idea of disarming the soldiers who guarded them, forging those terrible weapons of the Polish insurrections—scythes planted as pikes on long poles—and

making their way across the mountains and across
Mongolia, towards China, where they would find
English ships to take them.   One day the news came
to Irkútsk that part of those Poles who were at work
on the Baikál road had disarmed a dozen soldiers and
broken out into revolt.   Eighty soldiers were all that
could be despatched against them from Irkútsk.
Crossing the lake in a steamer, they went to meet the
insurgents on the other side of the lake.

The winter of 1866 had been unusually dull at
Irkútsk.   In the Siberian capital there is no such
distinction between the different classes as one sees in
Russian provincial towns ; and the Irkútsk ' society,'
composed of numerous officers and officials, together
with the wives and daughters of local traders and even
clergymen, met during the winter, every Thursday,
at the Assembly Rooms.   This winter, however,
there was no ' go ' in the evening parties.   Amateur
theatricals, too, were not successful ; and gambling,
which was usually pursued on a grand scale at Irkútsk,
only dragged just along : a want of money was felt
this winter among the officials, and even the arrival of
several mining officers did not bring with it the heaps
of bank-notes with which these privileged gentlemen
usually enlivened the knights of the green tables.   The
season was decidedly dull—just the season for starting
spiritualistic experiences with talking tables and talka-
tive spirits.   A gentleman who had been during the
previous winter the pet of Irkútsk society on account
of the tales which he recited with great talent, seeing
that interest in himself and his tales was failing, now
took to spiritualism as a new amusement.   He was

clever, and in a week's time the Irkútsk ladies were mad over talking spirits. A new life was infused amongst those who did not know how to kill time. Talking tables appeared in every drawing-room, and love-making went hand in hand with spirit rapping. An officer, whom I will call Pótaloff, took it all in deadly earnest—talking tables and love. Perhaps he was less fortunate with the latter than with the tables ; at any rate, when the news of the Polish insurrection came he asked to be sent to the spot with the eighty soldiers. He hoped to return with a halo of military glory. ' I go against the Poles,' he wrote in his diary ; ' it would be so interesting to be slightly wounded ! '

He was killed. He rode on horseback by the side of the Colonel who commanded the soldiers, when ' the battle with the insurgents '—the glowing description of which may be found in the annals of the General Staff— began. The soldiers slowly advanced along the road, when they met some fifty Poles, five or six of whom were armed with rifles and the remainder with sticks and scythes ; they occupied the forest, and from time to time fired their guns. The chain of soldiers did the same. Lieutenant Pótaloff twice asked permission of the Colonel to dismount and to dash into the forest. The Colonel very angrily ordered him to stay where he was. Notwithstanding this, the next moment the Lieutenant had disappeared. Several shots resounded in the wood, followed by wild cries ; the soldiers rushed that way, and found the Lieutenant bleeding on the grass. The Poles fired their last shots and surrendered ; the battle was over, Pótaloff was dead. He had rushed, revolver in hand, into the thicket, where he found several Poles armed with pikes. He fired all his shots at them in a haphazard way, wounding one of them, whereupon the others rushed upon him with their pikes.

At the other end of the road, on this side of the lake, two Russian officers behaved in the most abominable way towards those Poles who were building the same road but took no part in the insurrection. One of the two officers rushed into their tent, swearing and shooting at the peaceful convicts with his revolver, badly wounding two of them.

Now, the logic of the Siberian military authorities was that as a Russian officer had been killed several Poles had to be executed. The court-martial condemned five of them to death : Szaramówicz, a pianist, a handsome man of thirty who was the leader of the insurrection ; Celínski, an ex-officer of the Russian army, a man of sixty, because he had once been an officer ; and three others whose names I do not remember.

The Governor-General telegraphed to St. Petersburg asking permission to reprieve the condemned insurgents, but no answer came. He had promised us not to execute them, but after having waited several days for the reply, he ordered the sentence to be carried out secretly early in the morning. The reply from St. Petersburg came four weeks later, by post : the Governor was left to act 'according to the best of his understanding.' In the meantime five brave men had been shot.

The insurrection, people said, was foolish. And yet this handful of insurgents obtained something. The news of it reached Europe. The executions, the brutalities of the two officers, which became

known through the proceedings of the court, produced a commotion in Austria, and Austria interfered
in favour of the Galicians who had taken part in the
revolution of 1863 and had been sent to Siberia.   Soon
after the Baikál insurrection the fate of the Polish
exiles in Siberia was substantially bettered, and they
owed it to their insurgents—to those five brave men
who were shot at Irkútsk, and those who had taken
arms by their side.

For my brother and myself this insurrection was a
great lesson.   We realized what it meant to belong in
any way to the army.   I was away ; but my brother was
at Irkútsk, and his squadron was dispatched against the
insurgents.   Happily, the commander of the regiment
to which my brother belonged knew him well, and,
under some pretext, he ordered another officer to take
command of the mobilized part of the squadron.
Otherwise Alexander, of course, would have refused to
march.   If I had been at Irkútsk, I should have done
the same.

We decided, then, to leave the military service and
to return to Russia.   This was not an easy matter,
especially as Alexander had married in Siberia ; but at
last all was arranged, and early in 1867 we were on our
way to St. Petersburg.

END OF THE FIRST VOLUME

Spottiswoode & Co. Printers, New-street Squrre, London

Lightning Source UK Ltd.
Milton Keynes UK
UKOW05f0947161216

290177UK00012B/228/P